SOMEONE WILL BE
WITH YOU SHORTLY

"It's no mystery why *O, The Oprah Magazine*'s Lisa Kogan is a beloved columnist. She's self-deprecating enough to be easily relatable, whimsical enough to be reliably entertaining, and clever enough to disguise a gut-socking revelation." —*Elle*

"Lisa Kogan might just be the Erma Bombeck of our generation. Sassy, blunt, and so damn true."
        —Kelly Corrigan, author of *The Middle Place* and *Lift*

"Kogan's riffs on motherhood, politics, relationships, and life itself are what we wish we'd said, only sharper and funnier. This is good stuff."
                        —*O, The Oprah Magazine*

"If Lisa Kogan didn't exist, Nora Ephron would have to invent her. In essays that disarm and delight, Kogan's take on contemporary living is as irrepressibly savvy as a Prada diaper bag, as reassuringly satisfying as a PB-and-J sandwich."   —*Booklist*

"In delectable bite-size essays, humor columnist Kogan casts an all-seeing eye on the annoying and hilarious idiosyncrasies of contemporary life."   —*Redbook*

"Her wry observations of everyday life will hearten you on your worst days, validate you on your best, and make you laugh any day at all. Buy it, if not to keep Lisa writing, then as an investment in your own happiness. God knows you deserve one fail-safe investment."
                —Martha Beck, author of *Expecting Adam* and
                                Finding Your Own North Star

"Lisa Kogan has a singularly humane stance as she makes comic sense of the annoying and baffling facts of life. The inventor of 'the dessert potato' has made me laugh for years—she's been a comfort, too."

—Amy Hempel, author of *The Collected Stories*

"Kogan delivers stylish and funny meditations on being a single mom, Rush Limbaugh, modern media, and much more. There's laughter here, sure, but this book winningly rises above comedy to reveal a moving love of life."

—*Time Out* (New York)

"Lisa Kogan is the intellectual and creative love child of Noël Coward and Loretta Lynn. *Someone Will Be with You Shortly* is a hilarious, honest, and tender chronicle of everyday life as most of us really live it. Lisa Kogan sings all the right grace notes with absolutely perfect pitch."

—Amy Dickinson, author of *The Mighty Queens of Freeville*

"Lisa Kogan's *Someone Will Be with You Shortly* is a delectable blend of wit, whimsy, pith, and poignancy. If David Sedaris were a girl (who'd had her pocketbook licked by a stranger on Lexington Avenue) this is the book he'd write."

—Evan Handler, author of *It's Only Temporary*

"I admit it. I'm a big, drooling Lisa Kogan groupie. I'd read the ingredients on a cereal box if I thought she'd written them. She is funny, wise, compelling, lovable, fallible . . . so a whole book by her? What heaven!!"

—Peggy Orenstein, author of *Waiting for Daisy*

"Lisa Kogan's *Someone Will Be with You Shortly* is like curling up with your best, crabbiest, kindest, wisest, most singular friend on earth."

—Peter Smith, author of *Two of Us: The Story of a Father, a Son, and the Beatles*

SOMEONE WILL BE
WITH YOU SHORTLY

Notes from a perfectly imperfect life

LISA KOGAN

HARPER

NEW YORK ● LONDON ● TORONTO ● SYDNEY

HARPER

A hardcover edition of this book was published in 2010 by HarperStudio, an imprint of HarperCollins Publishers.

HarperCollins books may be purchased for educational, business, or sales promotional use. For information please write: Special Markets Department, HarperCollins Publishers, 10 East 53rd Street, New York, NY 10022.

FIRST HARPER PAPERBACK PUBLISHED 2011.

Designed by Eric Butler

The Library of Congress has catalogued the hardcover edition as follows:
Kogan, Lisa.
    Someone will be with you shortly : notes from a perfectly imperfect life / by Lisa Kogan.—1st ed.
        p.   cm.
    ISBN 978-0-06-173502-8
    1. Kogan, Lisa. 2. Journalists—United States—Biography. I. Title.

PN4874.K645A3   2010
070.92—dc22
                                                            2009046580

ISBN 978-0-06-173503-5 (pbk.)

11 12 13 14 15 OV/BVG 10 9 8 7 6 5 4 3 2 1

For Jonathan, Julia, and Johannes Labusch

CONTENTS

A BRIEF HISTORY OF ME

I SUPPOSE YOU'RE WONDERING why I've gathered you all here today. Wait a second—who starts a book like that? Why am I suddenly channeling Agatha Christie? Okay, let's not panic. I can break set, I can shift gears.

Maybe something like this: Attention everyone who was ever mean to me at Alice M. Birney Junior High (that means you, Randy Herschman, Greg Silver, Judy McMahon). I have a word processor now, and I'm not afraid to use it. . .

My name is Lisa Kogan, and I'm a forty-nine-year-old single woman who maintains that life is a fragile bit of luck in a world based on chance, that Ruth Bader Ginsburg should be cloned, that Bernie Madoff is the devil, that nobody's grown a decent tomato since 1963. What else? I live in New York City because it's the only place that would take me. I work at *O* magazine, which sounds vaguely glamorous—but mostly involves explaining why I can't get tickets to *The Oprah Winfrey Show* for my podiatrist's cousin. I have spent the best years of my life growing out bangs, searching for a good bra, and wishing I were skinny. (Here's a tip for anybody who's

LISA KOGAN

looking to drop a few pounds: Wishing doesn't do it.) I don't
understand money, football, corporate culture, or the computer I'm typing on. I used to think the world wasn't all that
complicated—just add water and live—but along came AIDS
and crystal meth and Rush Limbaugh and I guess I grew up.
Still, I'm deeply nostalgic for that time when you had to walk
across a room to change channels and there was no such thing
as a spy satellite capable of spotting the precancerous mole on
my inner thigh.

Have I left anything out? Let's see, my recent apartment
renovation consisted of turning over the sofa cushions, then
realizing they looked better the other way. I think every
human being deserves a great mattress, a comfortable pair
of shoes, and a very smart shrink—the rest is gravy. It's
been a long time since I've believed in God, but now that
I've put that in print, I'm scared that this God I don't believe in will be mad at me. I get scared a lot. I'm scared the
ozone layer is disappearing. I'm scared one of those horrible
superstores will be coming soon to a neighborhood near me.
I'm scared my parents are getting old. I'm scared my upper
arms are getting flabby. I'm scared of lunch meat. And I'm
frightened to death of ambivalent men.

For a long time, I had a type: dark, intense, just a touch
remote—you know the ones I mean, right? They don't want
you, but they want to make good and sure that you want
them. At the end of most dates, there'd be a quick peck on
the cheek and a simple "Well, it was nice not getting to know
you." My hope was that this sort of man would fall in love
with me. My prayer was that I would get over him. My wish
was that we had never laid eyes on each other.

Then, just when I decided I could have a fine life as what the wickedly funny Wendy Wasserstein used to call a "bachelor girl," Johannes appeared with his slow-dance eyes and his easy laugh—and ever so gently, he crushed my resistance like grapes into Cabernet. Except for a couple of bouts of stomach flu and a few genuinely ugly arguments, there hasn't been a day in nearly seventeen years when I haven't wanted to inhale him.

But there's a twist.

In order to share custody of his son, Johannes lives on another continent. For those of you playing the home game, that would be eight-thousand miles, nine lost-luggage situations, and a six-hour time difference away. We are together roughly every two months—making us the envy of most of our married friends. But there's another twist.

Her name is Julia Claire Labusch—and she's our six-year-old daughter. It's a pretty name, don't you think?

When I was five months pregnant I dodged the name-question with my mother. "Gwynff," I said.

"Gwynff?" my mother repeated.

"That's right, I'm going to name your one and only granddaughter 'Gwynff.'"

Silence. "Is that an actual word?" she asked calmly.

"Yes, I believe it's Welsh for 'We're not telling people the name we've chosen,'" I answered with equal calm.

"Middle name?" attempting nonchalance.

"Nosferatu," attempting to preserve privacy of middle-name decision.

"Ava is a nice name," she said, floating a trial balloon.

"Yes, you've mentioned that," I said, bursting it.

"I mean, not that you have to go with Ava or anything . . . Lauren, Emma, Rachel, they all work."

"Gwynff," I said.

My mother and I go back nearly half a century. It took a lot of time, but I've trained her well. She no longer tells me my paintings hang too low or my hemlines hang too high. She doesn't suggest I get my head out of the clouds or the hair out of my eyes. In exchange for which I refrain from complaining bitterly that she served broiled chicken with a side of Birds Eye frozen green beans virtually every night from 1974 to the bicentennial. She doesn't throw my inability to parallel park at me, and I've quit addressing letters home to "the woman who forced me to wear a coat over my Halloween costume." We've managed to forgive each other's frailties, to accept that she's neurotic and I'm, well, even more neurotic. We understand that I will never wear anything that involves appliqué and she will never eat anything that involves calories. It's a fairly complex truce but it generally works for us, and when it doesn't, we moan to our respective shrinks and live to love another day. Others are less fortunate.

My friend Robin insists that the next time her mother decides to slip her phone number to a divorced orthodontist from Great Neck, she fully intends to fake her own death. I applaud Robin's creative problem solving and hereby volunteer to show up at her phony memorial service and repeatedly sob, "Oh, dear God, I guess all that blind dating finally did her in."

They say good fences make good neighbors, but I look at the mothers and daughters I know and find myself wondering if the fence must be electrified to keep one's mother from straying into dangerous territory. I kept thinking, will this little person who's currently occupying space in my uterus have to one day line the borders of her heart with razor wire to stop me from chipping away at her choice of laundry detergent and footwear? How do we keep from becoming trespassers in each other's lives?

I ask my mother about this, but all she says is that everything will be fine. She insists I'll know what I'm doing, and that if I don't, little Gwynff Nosferatu will train me. Her vague response annoys me to no end. I'm looking for some hard-core mothering here, for a Campbell's commercial in which we're wearing chunky hand-knit sweaters and sharing deep truths over piping hot bowls of tomato rice soup. I want her to brush my hair and call me Cookie and say the kind of things you read in Hallmark cards—but that's just not my mother's style, nor was it her mother's and, for better or for worse, I'm pretty sure it won't be mine, either. Instead, I'll leave Julia Claire irritating phone messages suggesting she switch laundry detergents and invest in better shoes. And because I'm a writer, I'll probably write her all the things that my mother has said to me over the years—if not in word, then in deed: Always try. Always care. Always believe in what you're doing. Always respect yourself. Always know that you are loved. And always remember how happy you made me just by showing up for the big dance.

There was a lovely old Warren Zevon song—"Mutineer," I think it's called—playing the morning Jules was born. The song is about rocking the boat and venturing into uncharted territory and bearing witness to a life outside your own. At least I think that's what it's about. To be honest, I couldn't hear very much above the sound of my own shrieking. "I can't take it anymore," I wailed. "Really, how much longer?" Andrei Rebarber, obstetrician extraordinaire, took a quick peek between my flailing legs and deadpanned in a voice that struck me as altogether too serene, given that I had just attempted to kick his face in, "Someone will be with you shortly." Story of my life, Doc, story of my life.

"Is that your husband?" the nurse asked, pointing to Johannes.

"No, he's my next-door neighbor's husband, but he's crazy in love with me. We're planning to kill her for the insurance money, then buy a villa somewhere in Paraguay," I snarled. And she seemed more or less okay with that.

The rest of this story is pretty standard stuff; Johannes and the nurses ordered yang chow lo mein from the noodle shop on Second Avenue, my friend Meg dropped by, shifts changed, I threw up, day turned to night, my friend Francesca dropped by, I begged her to grab a chopstick and stab me through the heart, and then a little after 3 A.M., out came the pink velvet bunny nose, soft butter pecan ice cream cone, floppy peony petal, juggle bug baby girl I thought I would never have.

Five days later, Johannes left for Zurich, and I learned that one of the exquisite ironies of being a parent is you get to stay up as late as you want, but all you want is to go to bed early. I also learned how little I know about raising another human being. (Here's a tip for anybody out there bringing up baby: Never refer to your vodka-and-tonic as "Mommy's pain-go-bye-bye juice.") But I'll tell you more about that later. I'll also be showing you how it really feels to date Javier Bardem, what it's like to spend a full month—just me and my expense account—living it up on the isle of Capri, and together we'll analyze whether a simple girl from Detroit can find true happiness by being slathered in the trappings of unimaginable wealth—unless of course Javier Bardem, my boss, or Harry Winston has some sort of problem with that.

My, how time flies when I'm doing all the talking. We're already up to the part where I have to end with some simple, albeit clever, albeit straight from the heart, phrase—something that says we're all in this together, something that leaves everybody feeling a little less crazy in a world where "something a little less crazy" isn't always easy to come by . . . if only I knew what that was.

$\mathscr{P}$IECE OF CAKE

WHEN JULIA TURNED ONE on a rainy night in April, her grandfather bought her a chocolate cupcake from the little bakery around the corner, which she dutifully mashed into her forehead as I sang "Happy Birthday to You" and her grandmother stood by with a soapy washcloth. My friend Leslie suggested this might just be the most pathetic affair she'd ever heard of, and asked what I intended to someday tell my little girl about her first party.

"I will tell her that I rented a farm with ponies and a Ferris wheel and a magician and a rainbow and fireworks and sixty-seven ballerinas. I will tell her that Springsteen sang and Elmo juggled. And I will tell her that the world was in such fabulous shape, President Gore decided he could afford to take the day off and help blow out the candle on her strawberry-pink buttercream layer cake." Leslie rolled her eyes.

Julia's second birthday was spent in bed with a stomach virus, but eventually I will show her clips from the Macy's Thanksgiving Day Parade and point out how wonderful it was to have thousands of well-wishers lining the streets to celebrate her entry into the terrible twos.

My plan was to keep this up until she hit her mid-forties, but when Jules was on the verge of becoming a three-year-old, I knew the jig was up. She had begun to question how I balance the demands of being an ice-skating superstar with my rigorous schedule as the northeast's only true fairy princess. She was also getting invited to more and more birthday parties. She'd embraced half a dozen Barney clones, dined on politically correct tofu nuggets, and received goody bags filled with bubble wands and Hello Kitty stickers. There was no way out of it—I'd have to throw a party.

Perhaps I should back up for a second and tell you about the last party I threw. The year was 1994. Kurt Cobain had just committed suicide. *Schindler's List* won the Oscar, and I was feeling ambitious. Not ambitious in the learn-a-foreign-language, volunteer-at-a-shelter, go-for-a-power-walk sense of the word, but ambitious enough to make dessert from scratch.

Of course, hindsight is always 20/20. In retrospect, it's easy to understand why you don't see more flambéing done in the home. But who would ever have imagined that something called cherries jubilee could singe so much off so many?

When the smoke cleared and the little flecks of grated orange rind settled, I knew I'd given my last get-together. If a hostess has to end the evening by assuring guests, "With any luck at all, your eyebrows will grow back, good as new," it's time to take the extra leaf out of the dining table and call it a night.

But then was then, and now I needed to pin the tail on the

goddamn donkey. I scoured Manhattan for a suitable venue and settled on a pretty little place called Moon Soup. It had a giant penguin in the window and "Hound Dog" on the sound system. But what hooked me was the promise that my one job was to show up and have a good time—they would take care of everything else. I knew I was perfectly capable of showing up. Hell, I've been showing up for things all my life—why, just the previous week, I'd made it to a mammogram, a pedicure, a memorial service, and a new-parents' tea at Julia's preschool. The question was, could I have a good time?

About the only thing I like less than giving parties is going to them. Suffice it to say that I am still digging out from the emotional carnage that was Jason Eisner's bar mitzvah. Still, we do things for our children that we wouldn't do for anyone else on earth (except possibly Clive Owen, but that's a whole other chapter). I once hokey pokeyed fifty-four times in a single afternoon because—believe me—when you hit on something that distracts a baby from teething pain, you're more than happy to put your left foot in, take your left foot out, put your left foot in, and shake it all about.

But I digress. You're probably wondering how the social event of the season finally turned out, whether the kids liked the pizza bagels and the grown-ups liked the crudi-tés, if everyone had a maraca to shake, a hand to hold, a balloon to pop. If I actually managed to find a bit of bliss, a shot of redemption, a few moments of pure, unadulter-ated joy in seeing my daughter serenaded by all the people she loves. Can a phobic party giver wrestle her neuroses to Moon Soup's padded floor mat and triumph?

Well, in a perfect world, I'd be able to say that I not only survived, I turned out to be the hostess with the mostest and a good time was had by most. But—on the off chance that you hadn't noticed—this is not a perfect world, so I'll tell you the truth: One kid threw up, two kids cried, Julia started asking if we could go home about forty minutes before it was over, my parents started asking if they could go home about forty minutes after it started, I barked at Johannes (the only thing that kept him from divorcing me during this ordeal is the fact that he'd first have to marry me), and the phrase "Please, God, let this stuff I just stepped in turn out to be apple juice" was evoked several times over the course of two and a half hours. But according to my friend Jan, who has three kids and knows virtually everything I don't, in toddler circles this constitutes a rollicking success.

So, my darling daughter, when you grow up I will tell you that your third birthday party was fantastic—because for the most part it really was. But I might also mention that it's a very fine thread that sutures us to our dreams. My dream for you will always be sixty-seven ballerinas, but I'm afraid reality is a frequently overwhelmed mother and an old Jewish couple from Detroit picking cupcake out of your hair on a rainy night in April. The truth is, Springsteen was booked, Bush was president, and my skating did not take six gold metals at the Helsinki Olympics. But here's one more truth: For a couple of seconds there, my mom and dad and you and me were the finest family in the world. We shimmered with closeness, we shut our eyes, we made a wish, and we blew those candles out.

MESSING WITH MY HEAD

AT FIRST, YOU THINK every detail will remain forever lodged in your memory. *It was a Saturday. I had toast and a tangerine for breakfast. My sweater was cobalt blue.* But with time and distance and a perceptive shrink, you begin the arduous process of moving on. You think you'll never forget, but you do—you must.

And still, the dreams come. In them, a kindly old healer—think Henry Fonda—hears of my suffering.

"It's been a nightmare for you, hasn't it?" he whispers.

Through tortured sobs, I manage, "Yes. Oh God, yes."

He takes my face in his weathered hands and he hurls his fury to the heavens. "That . . . butcher!"

This, my friends, is the story of a very, very, very bad haircut.

It all began one mild morning in February when I realized that I was about three and a half weeks past my "delightfully shaggy" look. It was only a matter of days before I'd start bearing an uncanny resemblance to my demented aunt

Ida, a woman who spent her final years insisting she once had a "quickie" with the guy from *Gunsmoke*. I needed to do something, but rather than visit my regular stylist, I opted to save a few bucks and wander into one of those "no appointments necessary" clip joints. The year was 2005. I was so very innocent.

My haircutter—a chain-smoking artiste in white jeans—was named Plawmphh. He said it, he spelled it, I swear I heard Plawmphh. In retrospect, it occurs to me that Plawmphh may not have actually understood a whole lot of English, and that perhaps in the land of Plawmphh's birth, the phrase "Just take an inch or so off the ends" was phonetically indistinguishable from "Please, fuck up my life beyond all recognition."

Don't panic, I thought. *It's just hair,* I thought. *I'll be fine,* I thought. But I wasn't fine. My mojo was shot. And what began as a crummy haircut morphed into a seventeen-month-long lousy streak. Allow me to share a few highlights:

- Three days after the fatal haircut, on the way to a much-needed eyebrow and upper-lip waxing, I ran into my ex-boyfriend and his adorable young wife. Had I not been so flustered, I could have avoided the entire episode by insisting I was Gene Shalit. It was later brought to my attention that I also had a quarter-size patch of macaroni and cheese encrusted on my T-shirt.

- They discontinued my favorite lipstick. It was called Peach Melba and it made me look thin.

- Half of my health insurance claims were rejected, and the woman reviewing my case had all the intellect and people skills of Ann Coulter on a bottle of Nyquil.

- I could no longer enter a supermarket without ending up in the cash only, ten items or less line behind a guy who was attempting to pay for eleven cartloads of Toaster Strudel with a personal check from the Bank of Kabul.

- My daughter and I inadvertently moved into a Sutton Place building that's brimming with pretentious snobs. If anyone currently living in my building is reading this, I don't mean you . . . you're fabulous and I'm not the least bit offended every time you let the elevator door close in my face as I approach with a bag of groceries in one arm and a first-grader in the other. I'm not going to name names, but—oh hell, what's the point of having your own book if you can't use it against people who snap at your child in the lobby? You, Geraldine Cutler, are the human equivalent of biting tinfoil.

- A man on Seventy-fourth Street and Lexington Avenue licked my pocketbook.

- My former gynecologist asked me for tickets to *The Oprah Winfrey Show*. It's true, as I said earlier, somebody is always wanting *Oprah* tickets from me, but this particular request came—I kid you not—mid-Pap smear.

I understand why one might invoke the name of Betty Ford during a drug intervention—I can even see mentioning Katie Couric's name during a colonoscopy—but aren't there laws against making *Oprah* references while addressing a person in stirrups and a gown made of paper towels?

- Two words: *bad oyster.* Although on the plus side, I did lose five and a half pounds in a mere fourteen hours.

- In the past year and a half, I have broken my watch, oven, dishwasher, smoke detector, TV, DVD player, computer, iPod, humidifier, vacuum, and toe.

The truth is, I realize being cursed with crooked bangs probably hasn't got much to do with why I can't catch a break on line at the A & P. I even know that in the grand scheme of things, none of these irritants amount to very much but, you see, it's the grand scheme of things that is keeping me up at night.

Maybe this isn't the story of a bad haircut after all (though, so help me God, it looked like I'd been mauled by an ocelot). Maybe this is about the feeling that we're all living in a world gone off its rocker. We're watching families try to exist on a wage of $7.25 an hour, we're waiting for the next terrorist attack, and, to top it all off, the planet is melting. It doesn't really matter that a lunatic French-kissed my Marc Jacobs bag, or even that my gynecologist's timing was absurdly off. What matters is that we're witnessing the death of civility, and—if I remember anything at all from ninth-grade history—that's generally followed by the fall of civilization.

There is a quiet but constant undertow, a dull persistent ache that's with me all the time, and I don't think I'm alone. It's gotten increasingly weird out there, and so we turn inward. It's easier to think about hair than to think about North Korea, to blame some guy in white jeans rather than political or economic forces I can't begin to comprehend. I read the paper with a feeling of impotent rage. I worry that my daughter won't have the same rights my mother's generation fought for me to have.

But then I see Julia's face, and to quote the Monkees, I'm a believer. I believe that for every nasty claims adjuster putting me on hold, there's a sympathetic one willing to hear me out; that for every Geraldine Cutler in the lobby, there's a wonderful Wendy Goldstein just down the hall; that my ex's new bride probably has one of those screwed-up toenails that prevents her from wearing sexy sandals; that more and more people are making some righteous noise about our addiction to oil, paying attention to the climate crisis; that instead of praying for an end to war we're demanding it. I believe that we're finally starting to pause long enough between denial and despair to begin actually addressing our problems. And I cling to the belief that even the worst haircut eventually grows out.

4

ℳARGARET HAS SPOKEN

SHE THINKS I NEED a better bra, a lighter workload, a man with money. If she were my mother, I would have to strangle her. But she is not my mother; she is Margaret Forbes, the finest saleswoman on the face of the planet. "What are you, insane? Take that off immediately! The color, the shape— you look like a tea bag!" Margaret has spoken, and Margaret is right. "So," she says, making herself comfortable on the little bench in the corner of my dressing room, "I'm ready."

We've been down this road a time or two before. I know what's required of me. Reaching in to the slouchy suede bag Margaret insisted I buy four seasons ago ("You'll wear it for the next four seasons"), I take out the latest batch of pictures my daughter grudgingly sat for. It goes without saying that I'll be looking at her grandchildren, Robert, Michael, and Lauren, when I get to the cash register. She oohs and aahs over Julia, announces that she's available for babysitting seven nights a week, and hands me a black cashmere jacket to try. "Here, darling, it'll work with everything." Margaret has spoken and Margaret is right.

In most great love stories—*Anna Karenina, Marjorie Morningstar, Old Yeller*—the participants tend to remember every exquisite detail of their first meeting: who spied whom across a crowded room, the song that was playing, the faint scent of Shalimar wending its way through the air. But my first time with Margaret was probably pretty mundane. If I had to guess, I'd say she noticed me hauling a stack of sweaters around and decided to take pity. However it started, I left Saks Fifth Avenue that afternoon as the proud owner of two blouses, a pair of pants, a pencil skirt, and the sense that I could go anywhere dressed in some combination of the above.

Soon the seduction began in earnest; a handwritten note announcing the spring collection. A call that the outfit I'd been eyeing had just gone on sale, an invitation to a lunch for my favorite designer. Margaret made it her business to learn about the clothes in my fantasies and the clothes in my closet. She knew what I could afford to skip: "Won't your taupe linen top serve almost the same purpose?" And she knew what I had to have. "Nothing is making you happy today because you feel fat. But I'll be holding this dress for you until the middle of next week—at which time you are going to want it." She taught me to pair my silk charmeuse skirt with my denim jacket, that heels are a must, that anyone who looks good in ocher will look even better *not* in ocher.

I've seen Margaret command respect from the haughty and elevate the insecure, accessorize the clueless, and sweet-talk the seamstress. She is a diplomat and an advocate, a troubleshooter and a problem solver. She consoles, she motivates, she follows up. She knows how to alchemize tragedy into comedy, turn a bad date into a good story. And, so help me God, if Obama decides not to seek a second term— I'll single-handedly mount a campaign for Margaret Forbes to become the next president of the United States. I don't know about you, but I believe that the very least the leader of the Free World should be able to do is make me look thin.

But having now told you how I worship at her Joan & David–clad feet, that we are as close as two people can be, given that one needs to meet her sales quota and the other needs to pay her mortgage, I will tell you that Margaret and I are not actually friends.

As technology envelops us all in an ever-tightening chrysalis devoid of the most basic human contact, I find I make new friends about as easily as Europeans make ice cubes. But that's okay because—between working five days a week, freelancing on weekends, and raising Julia—I don't actually have time for the friends I've already got. No, Margaret is something different.

They say that centuries ago, people roamed the earth in familial tribes, that eventually they scattered to the winds, but now and then you come across someone, a kindred spirit, who's out there every day, just like you, attempting to earn a living, and fall in love, and get to the gym, and return a call, and hand-wash her delicates, and touch another life. Sometimes a look is exchanged. You stop for a second and say something—"Can you believe that guy?" or "This has been the worst allergy season in years" or "I'd kill to have hair your color"—and a face in the crowd becomes a face you recognize, a face you look forward to seeing in the neighborhood. Then, little by little, that face becomes a person who anchors you, who nourishes you, who opens up the world for you. Margaret is a member of my tribe.

New York City is not for the faint of heart. For one thing, it is a very expensive place to live. The price for every single activity—whether it's sending your child to nursery school or buying a cappuccino or parking in a garage—is $11,000. It is not uncommon for couples to run through their entire life's savings simply by going out for Thai food and a movie. This fact, combined with the pollution, the noise, the constant threat of another terrorist attack, and the knowledge that there is always an episode of *Law & Order SVU* being filmed in front of your supermarket (Mariska Hargitay has made it damn near impossible for me ever to pick up English muffins and a box of Cascade), tends to make most New Yorkers a touch snarky. They will interrupt their very important cell phone conversation to snort derisively and inquire as to the state of your mental acuity should you take more than six seconds to order your $11,000 cappuccino. I've been cursed at, bodychecked, and left for dead all because I got the last throw pillow at a Jonathan Adler sample sale. I've been flipped off, ripped off, and taken the long way home by every cab driver in midtown. I've been spilled on, growled at, shoved aside, and woefully misinformed from Soho to Central Park. Make no mistake; New York is hard, the world is cold, and there are days when life is just plain brutal. But I'm still here. And so is Margaret.

Marian, Lucy, and Jaime—the people who sneak Julia oatmeal cookies from behind the counter of the tiny gourmet shop on First Avenue—are also around. So is Mr. Thomas, who lives upstairs and knows all there is to know about theater. And then there's Jed, who stops to say hello each morning as he walks Spartacus (his mighty Chihuahua) past my bus stop. The truth is, I wouldn't dream of calling on any of these people if I were in trouble, nor would any of them come running to me. But we *could* and we know it. Which brings us back to Margaret.

"Sweetheart," says the voice on my answering machine. "I haven't seen you in ages. Did you decide which summer camp you're sending Julia to? Does she like gymnastics? Isn't your boyfriend back from Zurich this week? Call when you have a second to let me know that everything is fine. Oh, and I saw your last column. You are a very talented person, but white is not nice next to your face." And with one fifteen-second message, I feel . . . what? Loved? Sort of. Grounded. Sure. Part of a larger picture? Absolutely.

$\mathcal{M}$ EN: HOW AND WHY?

I'VE DONE A LOT of things for men. I have been waxed, pedicured, and (God help me) platinum blond for men. I have tried meditation, medication, tennis, chess, golf, poker, laser tag, and escargots for men. I have relocated, reproduced, and reinvented myself on more than one occasion for men. I have seen the films of Jackie Chan, read the poetry of Charles Bukowski, and learned the finer points of the Indianapolis 500 for men. I have rearranged my life for men, stuck to my guns for men, stood up for men, and gone down for men. I have lived for men and I have lived in spite of them.

But somewhere between the snails and the childbirth, I got a little tired of trying to figure out exactly what it is that men want from women. The real question is, What do women want from men? It just so happens that I, Lisa Kogan, am an actual living, breathing, water-retaining member of the female species (please see author's photo on cover), and have been for years. So allow me to throw out a few ideas:

- We want (and it's nothing short of remarkable that I'm saying this in the year 2010) to make the same money men make when we do the same job. And while I'm taking care of business, we want people either to quit telling us how essential it is that we breast-feed or start providing places where we can pump milk without fear of bumping into that guy who's making 30 percent more than we are for doing the same job.

- We want high heels that do not leave us praying for the sweet release of death.

- We want foreplay.

- We want a lot of foreplay.

- We want safe, reasonably affordable, fun, warmhearted day care for kids.

- We want peace, love, and understanding, but we also want red wine, compassionate lighting, and the occasional cheap thrill.

- We want all rock stars over sixty (I'm talking to you, Rod Stewart, Mick Jagger, Paul McCartney) to date women over sixty. Gentlemen, the day will come when you'll be needing a hip replacement. And— mark me—the moment your little friend can't be there for you because she's got Gymboree, my aunt Selma will seem like a slice of heaven.

- We want to stop being forced to watch *The Godfather* every single time it airs. The movie is a masterpiece. "Leave the gun, take the cannoli, blah, blah, blah." It's brilliant. We get it. Move on.

- Every now and again, we want somebody else to pick the restaurant, arrange the playdate, plan the seating, buy the tickets, do the laundry, schedule the appointment, pack the bags, balance the books, send the gift, walk the dog, fill out the forms, break the silence, lift the ban, make the payment, count the calories, hold the phone, explain the joke, beat the odds, hit the ground running, win the race, and save the day while we sleep past noon beneath high-thread-count sheets and a cashmere blanket. In other words, we want time off for good behavior.

I'm getting time off right now. Johannes and Jonathan, my sixteen-year-old stepson (it's been decided that I can call him stepson because though Johannes and I are not married in the eyes of the law, we have privately vowed to irritate each other for as long as we both shall live), are out seeing the kind of movie you couldn't convince me to watch even if it were playing inside my contact lenses, but it makes Jonathan happy and gives me a chance to hang out with my kid. At this point, you know all about Julia Claire—forty-six pounds of solid quirkiness—so it's time you meet the guys.

Jonathan is a citizen of the world. His well-traveled mother has taken him everywhere from Sri Lanka to Mexico. He is an authority on *The Colbert Report*, Sudoku, and soccer. He likes his pizza plain, his ice cream chocolate, his vegetables limited. He is a sworn enemy of anything that smacks of phoniness. He has never suffered fools gladly, met a guitar he didn't want to play, a pool he didn't want to dive right into. He listens to the Red Hot Chili Peppers, Linkin Park, Black Stone Cherry. He adores Jack Black, Will Ferrell, and Monty Python, but nobody makes him laugh harder than his father. After his grandfather's funeral, he asked me for a piece of gum, said a little prayer, knelt down, and placed it on the grave. I loved him so much at that moment, my knees nearly buckled. He is a wild child, frustrated and fragile, complaining and consoling, sweet-natured and fierce-tempered. He is a loyal friend, an old soul, a competitive player, a pure pleasure. And, as of last spring, he is officially taller than me.

Johannes knows every sad song Tom Waits ever recorded, every case Columbo ever solved, every homeless guy on the street. He can repair a broken DVD player, a torn coloring book, a bruised ego. He reads Rilke, he roasts chicken, he collects absurdities, he finds my mouth in the dark. He doesn't play devil's advocate, doesn't raise his voice, doesn't miss a trick. He loves smart design, worn-in boots, and me . . . sometimes not even in that order. He has the good manners that come from being raised by good people. He speaks three languages, raises interesting children, trusts his instincts, worships David Sedaris, Alberto Giacomettti, Rachel Maddow. He writes gorgeous music, brings home cherries in January, rides the roller coaster of my moods, stays when it'd be so much easier to go. If we ever split up, it will be due to irreconcilable similarities. So it's true—I've done more than my fair share for men (the laser tag alone should have qualified me for some sort of rehab), but at the end of the day, I know a couple of guys who do quite a lot for me.

6 .

$\mathscr{A}$DVICE FROM "A TERRIFIC GAL"

I SPENT A DOZEN Thanksgivings volunteering in a Harlem soup kitchen because—hell, I'll just say it—I'm one of the few women of my generation who look really good in a hairnet. Also, I love to cook. I love turning nothing into something. I love the smell of garlic and lemon and ginger and onion. I love how blissed-out a table full of people get over a crumbly cornbread stuffing or a perfectly dressed salad or a sweet potato–bourbon pie made from scratch. Oh, and there's one more reason I went out of my way to spend every holiday surrounded by a group of strangers: I couldn't bear to be with my family.

It's not that I don't love them—I do. They are a decent, God-fearing lot who would walk a mile out of their way to help if they thought you were in trouble. They recycle, they vote, they pay taxes, they e-mail the warning signs of a stroke. They are pillars of their communities, credits to their race, sugar and spice and everything nice, the cat's pajamas, the monkey's espadrilles. They'll meet your plane, they'll walk your dog, they'll remember your birthday, they'll save you a drumstick. But here's where my family and I parted company: They were all married with children, and for the first forty-two years of my life, I was neither.

One of these things is not like the others. One of these things just doesn't belong, goes the lyric to my favorite *Sesame Street* tune. Who'd have guessed that Big Bird would end up killing me softly with his song, but it's true—while I hardly qualify as the family's black sheep, in the race for odd duck I've broken away from the pack and am currently maintaining a significant lead.

Here's where I should remind you that Johannes lives in Switzerland and, as I've mentioned, Jules wasn't born until I was in my forties. I've looked at life from both sides now, but with my boyfriend off raising his son in Zurich eight months of the year, I continue to live with one foot planted firmly in the land of the single woman. And I'm here to tell you that it's hard out there for me and a whole lot of other bachelor girls in their thirties and forties.

I'm not entirely sure why I never married. I've been accused of being too picky, too career-oriented, too selfish, too difficult. If too picky means that I happen to be partial to men who chew with their mouths closed, then by all means, color me picky, but know that that's not only offensive, it's inaccurate. Hell, I'd have dated Ted Bundy if he were willing to meet in a well-lit, public place. No, I suspect it was your description of his "slight comb-over" and "profound desire to one day shake Dick Cheney's hand" that made me release that "catch" back into the wilds of New Jersey.

As for the rest, frankly I've always found myself to be utterly delightful (or at least no more ambitious, selfish,

difficult than any of my married friends). Still, in the interest of fairness, I invite those with opposing viewpoints
to go ahead and vent away in *their* books.

So what did happen? Is it possible that, like the dizzy
comic-strip women in those Roy Lichtenstein paintings, I
simply got too caught up in the little psycho-dramas of everyday living? Here's a thought: Maybe I was so busy dealing
with all my family's and friends' weddings that I didn't have
time for one of my own. I checked registries and bought
the silver seafood forks, the ice cream makers, the Tiffany
corncob holders, the lacy black camisoles for three dozen
bridal showers where I drank Prosecco and made nice to
the groom's aunt from St. Paul. I walked down the aisle in
satin pumps dyed Kit Kat—bar brown to match the strapless taffeta dress I was assured I'd wear again and again. I
sat through the toasts to couplehood, the questions about
when it would be my turn, the casual mention that "it's
perfectly okay to be gay . . . you know . . . if anybody happens to be." I smiled gamely as the band played "Someone
to Watch over Me." I threw sachets of politically correct
birdseed, and I went home and waited for the baby showers
to begin.

Evidently, nothing leads to pregnancy faster than owning
a set of Tiffany corncob holders, because it wasn't long
before I was buying the newlyweds a car seat, a crib set, a
soft yellow squeaky thing that played "Twinkle, Twinkle,
Little Star," and listening to brand-new mothers extolling
the virtues of a good epidural. Legend has it that my friend
Brenda found herself licking the anesthesiologist's fingers
during the birth of baby number three, but I'll save that for

my Valentine's Day chapter on unrelenting pain. Meanwhile, back at the Thanksgiving table, my list of cousins was growing. The holidays became about Sippy Cups and I became "the kid with the interesting job."

The only someone to watch over me was me, and everybody knew it. Conversational gambits at holiday dinners were confined to safe subjects guaranteed not to draw any attention to the fact that I'd never be on the receiving end of a silver seafood fork. Allow me to elaborate:

UNCLE SOL: Say, did you know that Dalmatians tend to be hard of hearing?

ME: Umm, no.

UNCLE SOL: It's true.

ME: Okay.

UNCLE SOL: So (*long pause*), how's your bicycle doing?

ME: Pretty good . . . yours?

UNCLE SOL: Great.

ME: Great.

They tried, I tried, we all tried, and the harder we tried, the more strained it got, until one day I had a baby of my own, and suddenly my relationship with Johannes was deemed legitimate and motherhood took me from screwup to grown-up in the eyes of the people whose respect I craved most.

That was a few years and a million somebody elses ago. Jules is in first grade now—and (as I write this) still single, though she has been seeing one Mr. C.J. Adler, who has not only lost three teeth but was recently awarded a medal for swimming with his face in the water.

I know that someday soon my girl will come home with a construction-paper Pilgrim hat and a pipe-cleaner turkey and they will become the centerpiece for our own Thanksgiving dinner, complete with our own traditions. We will invite all our friends who, thanks to divorces and long distances and family dynamics, find themselves free that night. We'll raise our glasses and drink to being who we want to be. And then we'll sit down to a large platter brimming with fettuccine Alfredo and all the trimmings. Once an odd duck, always an odd duck.

Having said all this, I feel compelled to remind my family and friends that I am a gainfully employed, God-fearing, law-abiding citizen, and I come in peace. I don't bet on baseball, I take excellent care of my gums, I keep my tray table locked and upright from takeoff to landing. And as if all that weren't enough: In spite of the boyfriend and the baby girl, I am *still* what is commonly referred to in polite society as an unmarried woman. As such, I am more than qualified to give you a crash course in the things one must never think, say, or do when dealing with a single woman.

1. Hey, cousin Christy, how 'bout we break with tradition and dispense with that bridal bouquet toss? Believe it or not, it's actually a touch degrading to be shoved front and center next to your spinster aunt

Mitzi from Winnipeg as a roomful of revelers hopped up on champagne and jumbo shrimp chant, "You're next, you're next."

2. Don't confuse being unmarried with being eleven. My love of SpongeBob-shaped macaroni and cheese not-withstanding, I never wanted to sit at the children's table. Nor did I want to ride in the backseat with your darling toddler, his pet tarantula, his Spider-Man glitter glue, and his melting Fudgsicle.

3. Kindly stop filling every conversational lull by announcing how much you love Ellen DeGeneres. Again, being single is not the same thing as being gay. Just as being married is not proof of being straight . . . but I'll explore that concept more fully in my "Uncle Barry's Very Special Friend" chapter.

4. I honestly don't care if your marriage is so toxic in its dysfunction that it makes the couple from *Who's Afraid of Virginia Woolf?* looks like Will and Jada—I'm not here to judge. All I ask is that you quit judging me. Has it ever occurred to you that single women and men are not suffering a fear of intimacy as much as a fear of being trapped in a crummy marriage?

5. Enough with the "constructive" criticism already. We live in a world of stunning technological advancement, but it remains physically impossible to wear your heart on your sleeve *and* be emotionally distant, dress like a

slut *and* a librarian, try much too hard *and* not make any real effort.

6. New rule: You may discuss everything from the fall of the Roman Empire to the rise of Rem Koolhaas with your single friend. But her uterus, ovaries, in fact, her entire reproductive system are off-limits. Sending clippings about a seventy-four-year-old Ukrainian woman who just gave birth to triplets along with a peppy little "Keep hope alive!" Post-it note will do irreparable damage to your relationship and—if the woman is particularly resourceful—may even get your tires slashed.

7. Here's a phrase that must never, *ever* cross your lips: "Let me tell you why a terrific gal like you is still single . . ." Because you see, that "terrific gal" is likely to have read one of those stories you come across every so often about people who don't have the guts to commit suicide and wind up provoking a cop into shooting them. It's easy to see how she could then interpret "Let me tell you why a terrific gal like you is still single" as code for "Please come up quietly behind me and bludgeon me to death."

8. Here is the truth: Single women are not Sarah Jessica Parker in *Sex and the City* any more than we're Glenn Close in *Fatal Attraction*. For one thing, very few of us have Manolo Blahniks in our closets. For another, very few of us have sex with Michael Douglas in our

kitchens. We sometimes get lonely, frustrated, we sometimes get flat-out goofy. We are human beings— tickle us and we laugh, prick us and we bleed, offer us rigatoni and we eat . . . in other words, we're pretty much like all of the married women I know.

7

Julia Has Three Mommies

THE LOVE OF MY life is seeing other women. It started inno-
cently enough, a bite to eat, a stroll through the park—the
stuff I never have time for. Then came the private jokes, the
pet names, the stolen kisses, the bubble baths. At first I was
crushed. What did these women have that I didn't? Sure,
they're gorgeous, but I happen to look very nice in navy;
and yes, they're bright, but I scored unbelievably high on
the SATs . . . if you don't count the half with all that math. I
told myself it was just a fling, but a blind man could see that
wasn't the case.

The truth is this: My daughter would follow Miranda Dedushi and Lidra Basha, her two babysitters, to the ends of
the earth, and the feeling is more than mutual.

For a while, I worried that with Julia's grandparents so
far away and Johannes living in Europe for long stretches,
Julia's world would be pitifully small, but then along came
Miranda and Lidra with their Kosovar lullabies and hair-
braiding expertise, and everyone's life took a major turn for
the better.

They say you can't pick your family, but Jules and I would beg to differ. I spent a lot of time picking caregivers who would cherish and respect my little girl, and, as a result, my little girl fell head over heels for both of them. To be honest, I was afraid she preferred them, that because I'm in an office all day, she wouldn't understand I was the one who pulled her through the croup of 2004, the one who managed to score last-minute Dora the Explorer at Radio City Music Hall tickets, the one who taught her to quit putting grapes in her ear. It turns out I needn't have been concerned. She gets it. Kids have a way of figuring this stuff out. They have a primal understanding of who their mother is—but what about the aunts and uncles, the cousins, the brothers and sisters, the people who give you a place in the world . . . and occasionally drop a gummy worm down the back of your T-shirt just for good measure?

My aunt Molly was my grandmother's youngest sister. Maybe Molly and her five siblings were a touch touchy, but after being on the receiving end of several rather unpleasant pogroms, they began feeling somewhat less than welcome in Russia. So in 1919, they made their way to Detroit, where my aunt Molly met and married my uncle Clyde, a good solid soul from (I'm not kidding) Tightfit, Tennessee, and gradually became the family matriarch . . . which is to say she had a swimming pool in the yard and filled it with cousins every summer. My aunt Annie would show up with homemade elderberry wine, though my uncle Izzie preferred to lounge poolside with a tall glass of pickle brine as my brother and cousins and I looked on in horror. My uncle Sam quoted Shakespeare, and my aunt Minnie did needlework. Everybody argued in Yiddish and laughed and snuck scraps of brisket to the dogs hanging out under the picnic table. I loved those days and I loved those people, but they're all gone now, and Sunday afternoons are for running errands. Julia never did have the pleasure of their company.

Still, I know that in years to come, my daughter will remember eating Albanian cabbage pie with Lidra's parents (whom she calls Miss Mommy and Mr. Daddy) and summer evenings at the Botanical Gardens with Lidra and her sister and brothers. Jules will look back at trips to the Bronx Zoo with Miranda and her husband and realize that—just like her mother—she comes from a great big, slightly offbeat, seriously funny family who would literally do anything for her.

Now, I'd gladly leave it at that, but I can't very well talk about the village it takes to raise Julia without talking about the e-mail that came across my desk yesterday. You see, I mentioned earlier that one of the things people need most is good, reasonably affordable day care for their kids. I even wrote about it in *O* magazine. Here is the response I got from a thirty-something Nebraska woman: "I have great news for Lisa Kogan—safe, affordable, fun, warm-hearted day care for kids does exist. It's called parents. By actually raising the children we choose to bring into the world, we can give our kids all this and more."

Oh, Miss Nebraska, what am I going to do with you? The old me would've simply ignored your "great news" (if one considers consuming 33 Mint Milano cookies, 2 Snapples, and a 6.6-ounce bag of those little Cheddar Goldfish "ignoring"), but a funny thing happened on the way to turning forty-nine: I took a deep breath and decided I'm much too old and way too tired to keep nursing my adolescent obsession with being loved. The need to please has at long last atrophied and set me free. So, lady, this one's for you:

I will resist a smart-ass reply congratulating you on being one of the eleven remaining members of society who can get by on a single income, especially given the forecasts that in the year 2021 (when my daughter is ready for college), four years at a public institution will run somewhere in the neighborhood of $129,788. And should Julia be smart enough to get into an Ivy League university, we're looking at roughly $279,760. Fortunately, she recently spent the better part of an hour with her little head stuck inside a shoebox, so affording Harvard may not be an issue. But I can't help thinking how incredible it must feel to be unfazed by this prospect. I envy people the ability to stay home with their kids, and there are plenty of days I wish I could be home with my daughter. Miss Nebraska, I, too, am a believer in quantity time, and I certainly agree that if you choose to bring a baby into this world, you'd better be prepared to raise it.

But I also think that there's more than one way to raise someone. Whether you're doing it alone or with a partner, raising a child may be a labor of love but, as anyone who's ever attempted to talk her daughter out of her American Girl doll obsession can tell you, it's still labor. So imagine my weariness when I picked up a magazine in the pediatrician's waiting room touting the virtues of a little something called "mommy time." Apparently the concept involves making a point of getting out there and enjoying a manicure, a movie, a long lunch with an old friend——it's all about making your-self a priority on a regular basis. But here's the thing: I took forty-two years for myself and today my priority is a Barbie backpack-carrying forty-six-pounder with a wobbly tooth and a tendency to wake up every Saturday at 5:45 A.M.

Who are these manicured mommies analyzing the latest indie flick over salad Niçoise? Are they the same women who do Pilates, run multimillion-dollar corporations, vol-unteer at nursing homes, and campaign for clean water while having soul-shredding sex with their adoring husbands four to seven times a week and twice on Sundays? Because I don't know any mommies like that. The women I know feel victo-rious when they manage to buy stamps. We're a motley crew all in serious need of a haircut and a shot of caffeine. Like the Marines, we do more before 9:00 A.M. than most people do in a day. We've seen things in diapers that would send most members of polite society shrieking into the night. There is no surface in our homes that doesn't feel sticky, no cushion on our sofa that hasn't been irrevocably stained. There is no part of our physical beings that hasn't been thrown up on. We live mostly on organic apple juice, chicken nuggets, and the edge . . . and that, for better or for worse, till sleepaway camp do us part, is mommy time.

The truth, Miss Nebraska, is that I've never really believed it's possible to have it all. But I know that with a strong sup-port system (i.e., nanny, sitter, grandma, day care, door-man who doesn't drink, or some combination of the above), you can have a career *and* a baby if that's what you need or want to have. Will that baby eventually become an adult who requires the services of a very wise shrink because you screwed up? Of course! That's what parents do, whether we work or stay home—we screw up. We try our damnedest, we love our hardest, and then we force them to wear a coat over their Halloween costume and all hell breaks loose. We want to be better than our parents were, and in certain ways we are better and in certain ways we're not.

But I don't want to fight with you, Miss Nebraska. I've had enough of red state/blue state, your God or mine, tastes great versus less filling. The planet is divided enough, so I'm officially calling for a cease-fire, a moratorium on snarkiness, a touch of tolerance. We are better than this—we are women. We crave potato products, we read witty novels, we notice shoes, we follow our gut, we try to keep men from becoming violent, we shop for bargains, we make sacrifices and quit our jobs to stay home and bring up our babies, or we make sacrifices and go to work and find other smart people to help us keep the plates spinning. It's all good, and it's all problematic, too. There is no right or wrong here, and that, Miss Nebraska, is just the way the cookie (which was not made from scratch, because, hey, this is 2010) crumbles.

8

𝒮UGAR SHOCK

LIFE CAN TURN ON a dime. One minute you're in your law-yer's office discussing the possibility of adoption, the next you're standing in your bathroom staring at a little stick that—against all odds—has somehow managed to register two skinny pink lines. Anyway, that's my story. I was forty-one years old, I was pregnant, I was cautiously euphoric. And then the world turned upside down.

It was September 24, 2002. Nearly three weeks after declaring me pregnant, the obstetrician sent a letter saying my glucose appeared "slightly elevated"; she suggested a glucose tolerance test "at my earliest convenience." Fed up with never once being able to get her on the phone, I called a colleague's husband, a highly respected obstetrician-gynecologist, and read him the results of the test. There was a pause—I remember that—and then I think he said some-thing like "Uh-huh, okay, hold on a minute while I make a call." After a very long minute, he got back on the line with what struck me as an absurd question. "Are you wear-ing shoes?" he asked. "Yep, I'm in my sensible pregnant-girl flats," I answered. "Good," he said. "I want you to grab your bag and get into a taxi. You'll be going to 168th Street and Saint Nicholas Avenue. Take the elevator to the . . ." It was going way too fast. "Listen," I said. "I'm pretty beat, but maybe tomorrow." And then he cut to the chase: "You're diabetic," he said, "and this baby can't wait until tomorrow." He explained that my soon-to-be-former doctor had taken much too long to diagnose me, and that, at nine weeks along, my baby's organs were being formed in an environment of uncontrolled sugar. He said other things, but it was all a blur. Thirty-five minutes later, I found myself at the place that would become my second home: Columbia University's Naomi Berrie Diabetes Center in New York City.

I have endured great pain in my day. A large woman named Helga waxes my bikini line every May, and I had a roommate who once listened to Enya for nine straight hours—so believe me when I tell you I understand human suffering, and I realize that in the grand scheme of things a little finger jab or an occasional shot in the arm doesn't really hurt all that much. But needles freak me out. It's irrational, it's phobic, it's not changing anytime soon. Before I could meet the doctor, I was to be given a hemoglobin A1C test—a simple finger stick that determines your average blood sugar for the past three months. "Not that hand, this one," I sobbed. "Wait, *this* finger. Use *this* finger. Hold it; I'm not ready," I pleaded as I breathed in the nauseating smell of rubbing alcohol on cotton. The little girl in the next chair rolled her eyes. A slightly more sympathetic preschooler assured me that "they're quite good here." It is not pretty when you're seated with two people under the age of seven and the only one who wants her mommy is you. Just then I felt a hand on my shoulder. "Hi, I'm Dr. Robin Goland. We'll sit down and talk in a couple of minutes," and in a futile effort to further reassure me, she added, "I promise you're not the first woman in history ever to be diabetic *and* pregnant." But I was pretty sure she was wrong. "Actually, Dr. Goland, I believe I'm the first woman in history ever to be pregnant."

Holding my newly pricked finger as if I'd been bayoneted, I settled in for a chat with Dr. Goland. She was a combo platter, equal parts wry, compassionate, and no-nonsense, a slim powerhouse in her late forties who I imagined cheerfully defusing a midlevel nuclear device while forging a permanent peace in the Middle East and harnessing solar energy. Over time I found out that she had absolutely no grasp of pop culture and once forgot her child at an ice rink, but this was only our first date. That day I needed her to be clear, kind, heroic—and that's exactly what she was.

To my total shock, the result of my hemoglobin A1C test indicated that my diabetes was not gestational. It proved that I was walking around with undiagnosed diabetes before ever becoming pregnant. Dr. Goland asked me about my family history (cancer galore). She asked me if I smoked (never). She asked me about my diet and fitness routine (used to see my trainer three times a week, currently see my refrigerator three times a night). Then it was my turn to ask the questions.

"What exactly happens if your blood sugar is too high?"

"Blindness, loss of limb, kidney failure, heart attack, stroke."

With each word I shifted deeper into catatonic noodle mode.

"But," she added, brightening, "every one of these things can be delayed or prevented. Because we didn't used to know how to keep blood sugar normal and how to prevent the complications, a lot of people are under the misconception that first you get the disease, then you get the problems, and that's that. The truth is, if you work to control it—and it is work—none of this is inevitable. You can be a healthy person with diabetes—you may never experience any of these complications."

My eyes scanned the room as I tried to take all of this in. There was a Harvard diploma hanging on the wall, pictures of three tanned tourist kids in front of some Greek ruins, a tiara-wearing teddy bear resting on the windowsill. I massaged my ever-expanding stomach and finally asked the million-dollar question: "Is my baby okay?"

Dr. Goland said it was too soon to tell. She wanted to send me to a lab so they could run more tests, and I started a fresh round of sobbing. Directing me to the nearest box of tissues, she stepped out of the room and returned followed by a band of angels. "You know what, Lisa, you don't need to get yourself to another lab. We're going to take some blood right now." Two nurses, Dr. Goland, and one vampire/medical assistant named Berenise ("She's the best") brought me into an examination room and started rolling up my sleeves in search of a good vein. It's a remarkable tribute to

SOMEONE WILL BE WITH YOU SHORTLY

peer pressure and vanity that I ever allowed my ears to be pierced, and I explained how that procedure actually made me pass out. They had me lie down, and the process began.

"So," said Dr. Goland, who seemed to believe in the power of distraction, "what's Rosie really like?" Through clenched teeth, I told her that I worked for Oprah and that though I'd never really said this to anyone before, "I guess the thing that makes Oprah so special to me"—they all leaned forward—"is that SHE'S NEVER STABBED ME IN THE ARM WITH A SHARP NEEDLE."

Dr. Goland decided I should be hospitalized till I got the hang of everything. I begged her to let me go home. "You'll have to test your own blood tonight and give yourself a shot of insulin," she said.

"I can do that," I said, almost certain that I couldn't do that.

"You'll have to call me at home tonight between ten and eleven."

"Okay," I answered, "if I need you, I'll call." She scrunched her brow. "I don't think you understand—if I don't hear from you, I'll be up worrying the entire night. You have to call."

Then she presented me with a secret weapon in my brand-new war. "This is Leigh Siegel-Czarkowski—you'll be spending a lot of time together."

I recognized her from my bloodletting.

"I'll walk you through the injection and blood test now, and then we can go over it again tonight," said Leigh, a thirty-something nurse-practitioner and diabetes educator, as she handed me her home phone number. I left the office at around 6:30 with a glucose meter, insulin pen, test strip, needle, lancet, and splitting headache. Only later did I learn that the office closes at 5:00.

That night I laid everything in front of me and phoned Leigh.

"I don't think I can handle this," I said, attaching the needle to the insulin pen.

"That's how I used to feel," she said, and instructed me to pinch my thigh.

"You're diabetic?"

"Since I'm fifteen."

"Leigh?"

"Hmmm."

"Isn't there some horrible disease I can get that involves ointment?"

"Of course there is," she assured me, "but right now you've got this."

I sank the needle into flesh, pushed the button on the pen, forced myself to count slowly to five until the drug was completely released, and pulled the needle from my leg.

"Leigh?"

"I'm right here."

We listened to each other breathe for a while and finally she said, "Let's stick your finger now so you can call Dr. Goland and say good night."

First thing the next morning, I was back in Leigh's office—a place I'd be hanging out in every day for hours over the next three weeks. We'd also talk at least twice daily on weekends. After conferring with Dr. Goland, it was decided that I would prick my finger to check my blood seven times

a day and control my sugar with five daily injections of insulin. Needless to say, I was not part of the decision-making
process.

A couple of weeks went by. I knew everyone and they knew
me. Needles, carb counting, weighing and recording every
bite of the three small meals and three small snacks that I
consumed at roughly the same time each day still didn't come
naturally, nor did willing myself to believe that I'd have a
healthy baby—but I did it nonetheless. Dr. Goland checked
my blood pressure, and in the peppy cheerleader style I'd
come to cling to pronounced me "completely amazing."

"Completely amazing people don't let themselves become
diabetic," I said.

Dr. Goland shot me the have-I-taught-you-nothing? look
and pulled up a chair. "This is not your fault, Lisa."

"C'mon," I said. "I've stopped going to the gym, I've put
on weight, I've—"

"Time out," she interrupted. "Diabetes is a genetic disease. And as for being overweight, that's one of the most
inheritable conditions we know of. Almost as much as
having blue eyes."

"Okay," I replied, "but you've gotta admit that there's an
environmental component to all this."

"Clearly there is. But in most cases, without the genes
you don't become diabetic. You could weigh four hundred
pounds, but if you don't have the genes, chances are your
blood sugar would be normal."

My eyes remained glued to the scale across the tiny room.

"I think it's a little unfortunate that we believe eating

is completely an issue of free will. It's not. Food intake is carefully regulated. It has to do with survival of the species. There are important circuits in the brain that are hardwired to direct how much we eat and when we feel satiated, and it's increasingly clear that there's a derangement, probably an inherited derangement, in the circuits of a person who struggles with weight."

And here I thought it was my needle phobia and constant weeping that would convince her I was deranged. "Now," she continued, "this isn't to say you couldn't go on a diet and lose weight after the baby is born—you could. It's just extremely hard to keep it off when the circuits are altered and your body is telling you you're hungry. It's also much easier for some people to gain weight. And again, that's their genes talking. The thing is, if you really pay attention and you're willing to be a little hungry and exercise regularly, your genes are not your destiny."

I vowed then and there never to touch spaghetti carbonara again.

"People who struggle with diabetes still have to live in the real world. It's unrealistic to tell someone they can never have the good stuff. If there's something you love to eat, I want to make sure you can still eat it from time to time. It's impossible to always be perfect. You have to learn what your blood sugar levels are supposed to be and keep them within those limits eighty percent of the time—shoot for a solid B; the other twenty percent is a quality of life issue."

And so, eight years later, I continue to eat a lot of vegetables, some protein, and an occasional dish of spaghetti. I walk home from the office at a fairly brisk pace two or three evenings a week, but the secret to my fitness program involves chasing around a funny little kid with a voracious curiosity and a mind-boggling level of energy. It took a village, but Julia Claire Labusch was born perfect and pink, healthy and happy—the most delicious sugar substitute I've ever come across.

9

𝒯HEY'LL ALWAYS HAVE PARIS

EVER HEAR THE ONE about the guy who had peachy-pink peonies imported from Chile every February? Apparently, he wanted to guarantee his sweetheart a touch of spring each morning. Then there's that story of the man who kept his wife's kindergarten picture in his wallet because they met on the first day of school and (even after sixty-six years together) that photo never failed to make him smile.

Oh, and let's not forget my personal favorite: This one involves a woman who thought her boyfriend was taking her for a weekend in East Hampton. Work was high-stress and they were both pretty beat. "You know what? I don't feel like driving," the man said casually. "Let's head for LaGuardia and catch a puddle jumper." But as they approached the airport, he announced a little change in plans. "You'll be needing this," he said, and put a passport in her hand. The very surprised woman and her boyfriend didn't go to the Hamptons that weekend. Instead, he jetted her off to Paris, and there, in the courtyard of the Louvre, he got down on one knee and proposed.

All three stories sound like urban boyfriend legends. But Peony Guy does exist—he colors my hair. And, yes, Virginia, somewhere outside Tucson there lives a seventy-one-year-old gentleman who is still madly in love with the girl who taught him to hopscotch. As for Mr. Ooh-La-La, I saw the engagement ring with my own two eyes and—so help me God—that diamond was bigger than my high school.

When I recount the tale of my friend's Parisian proposal to Johannes, there is a thoughtful pause. I know he must be doing what I did—picturing the giddy hand-in-hand walk along the Seine, the caviar on toast points at dinner, Notre Dame glowing against a blanket of stars in the night sky. I sigh. He sighs: "Hey, do you remember the time I went out and bought the stuff that turned the water in your toilet that cool ocean blue color?"

"Yeah, honey," I said, "I remember."

I am a sensible woman. I keep Bactine in my medicine chest, an umbrella in my office, $200 in my sock drawer. I'd sooner remove my own spleen with a grapefruit spoon than buy a set of sheets that require ironing. I favor practical shoes, low-maintenance hair, and whichever frozen peas happen to be on sale. I'm not entirely sure what a bodice is, but I can tell you that I don't want mine ripped. Still, I can't help feeling that there's something to be said for moons and Junes and Ferris wheels. I believe in the power of marabou, the brothers Gershwin, bubble baths in claw-footed tubs surrounded by a bazillion twinkly white candles. I believe in strawberries coated in dark chocolate and raspberries floating in pink champagne. I'm glad Victoria has a few secrets. I think fireplaces should be lit, compliments should be paid, *La Bohème* should be sung, legs should be shaved. I want Lassie to come home. I want Ali McGraw to live, and I want Gene Kelly to dip Cyd Charisse straight into next Thursday. I'm not proud of this, but in the interest of full disclosure, here it is: I am deeply relieved when Tom Hanks and Meg Ryan finally kiss. My name is Lisa, and I am a romantic.

The truth is that I fell for someone who prefers a blue toilet bowl to, oh, I don't know, let's say *Wuthering Heights*. Here is the worst (and by far the stupidest) fight Johannes and I ever had:

J: What are you reading about?

L: Ida and Isidor Straus. They were an amazing couple! Instead of getting into the lifeboat, she decided to die with her husband on the *Titanic*. Of course, if Julia were grown, I'd do the same for you.

J: What do you mean?

L: What do you mean, what do I mean?

J: You're not getting in the lifeboat?

L: No, I love you too much to let you drown all by yourself.

J: But I wouldn't be by myself—I think they were playing poker and getting drunk.

L: So you're saying that you'd rather play poker with John Jacob Astor than cuddle with me?

J: That's not what I'd be doing, because if you're not getting your ass into that lifeboat, then I am. We are not leaving an empty seat.

L: You're getting into that boat over my dead body.

J: Where the hell is the Tylenol?

L: Try the bathroom—you know, the place with the ocean blue toilet water.

J: You mean like the ocean you want both of us to sink to the bottom of?

Things kind of spiraled downward from there, and I still break into a cold sweat every time Celine Dion starts wailing about how her heart will go on.

So Johannes and I won't be taking a cruise together anytime soon. And no, those weren't his arms around me as I perched on a dune watching the sun come up over the Sea of Galilee; he wasn't the man who sent me a basket of French damson plums or the one who wanted all babies to have my nose. The slow dances are few and far between these days, and walks in the rain usually involve him running up ahead with the kid. But he did teach me how to fly a kite last summer, and we have been known to share steamed dumplings in a little East Village dive he discovered a few years back, and sometimes early in the morning I overhear him playing "tea party" with our daughter, and sometimes late at night I overhear him playing "Blackbird" with his guitar. He has genuine integrity, he has serious style, and he's pulled me through more than one bout of food poisoning. Anybody can sprinkle rose petals across a big brass bed, but only a real man will hold your hair while you're throwing up.

Now, there are those who will say that references to intense nausea don't belong in a meditation on romance, but I'm thinking maybe it's time we broaden our definition of what constitutes romance. Ask yourself this:

When the man you love realizes that half the screws are missing from the Ikea bookcase he's attempting to assemble for you, does he:

a. Complain bitterly about herring and Volvos—vowing to forsake all things Swedish for the rest of his natural days?

b. Leave the shelving in a heap on the living room floor and question your need to read in the first place?

c. Complete construction using a combination of rubber bands and Scotch tape while suggesting you fill the thing with pamphlets rather than actual books?

If you answered (c), then, my friend, life is good— because it means somebody out there loves you enough to try to get your bookcase together. That creative effort is the kind of everyday gesture on which great romances are built. I wouldn't be surprised to hear that while at the drugstore picking up the amulet of poison, Romeo also picked up a copy of *People* for Juliet. I like to imagine Abelard taping *30 Rock* for Héloïse. I bet a day didn't go by that Mel Brooks wasn't funny for Anne Bancroft.

Don't get me wrong. I'll always want the chubby little cupids and coconut bonbons, but lately I find myself drawn to something richer, deeper, sweeter—and a whole lot messier. Give me a poorly constructed bookcase . . . and each day is Valentine's Day.

10

ℳISS KOGAN REGRETS

Regrets, FRANK SINATRA CROONS over my ridiculously old JBL speakers. *I've had a few, but then again, too few to mention.* Which leads me to this conclusion: Ol' Blue Eyes never had to write a magazine column. If he did, he would know that when you're forced to fill a 1,300-word space twelve times a year, *everything* bears mentioning. I stand in the produce section wondering what a pomelo is and whether I can get a column out of it. I see a woman trip in front of Bloomingdale's and (instead of rushing to help her up) I begin spinning it into a piece on the perils of stiletto heels. Regrets? I've had a few, and I'll be more than happy to mention every last one of them if they'll fill a few pages.

{1976}

Rebellion rocks Soweto, America turns two hundred, Red Army Faction terrorists stand trial in West Germany, and I am an impressionable fifteen-year-old fresh from seeing the Streisand-Kristofferson remake of *A Star Is Born*. I regret thinking that if I permed my stick-straight hair to look like Barbra's, I could somehow become fabulous enough to snag Kris Kristofferson. Instead, I attend my first major make-out party looking as if a demented poodle had coiled itself around my head.

{ 1 9 8 4 }

John DeLorean is acquitted, the Apple Macintosh is in stores, *Miami Vice* convinces men to dress as if they were dishes of sherbet, and I am twenty-three years old, living in New York City. I regret that I didn't raise a little more hell back when I still had nothing to lose. But I got no kick from cocaine and mere alcohol didn't thrill me at all. I was born the old soul, the good girl, the designated soup schlepper, and I actually believed that I had the rest of my life to go out dancing in ruby red lipstick.

{ 1 9 8 9 }

Exxon screws up Alaska, Salman Rushdie irks the Ayatollah, Zsa Zsa Gabor slaps a motorcycle cop, and I leave a job in real estate that paid more money than I had ever made before (or since) to take a job as an assistant at a little weekly magazine called *7 Days*. I'm not sure that changing careers in my late twenties is a brilliant idea, but my father tells me that when you really love what you do, you tend to be pretty good at it, and when you're good at something, the money eventually comes. I regret that I never thanked my dad for saying what I needed to hear at the exact moment I needed to hear it. Only a few years earlier, he'd told me that it's always best to open the garage door *before* backing out of the garage. Now, that was a situation where he probably should have said something a little bit sooner than when we were standing in the driveway surveying what was left of the car and the garage. Anyway, it was at 7 *Days* that I met my friend Mark Carson—the person who taught me almost everything I know about grace and courage and authenticity.

{ 1 9 9 1 }

Anita Hill speaks truth to power, the Soviet Union calls it a day, the Gulf War begins, and it hits me that I'm looking for something I will never find with my boyfriend of nearly five years. The rites of passage are narrow and they come just once. If I hadn't walked away that ice-cold November morning, I know I'd have stayed for the rest of my life. I regret that it took me so damn long to figure out who I wanted to be when I finally grew up, and I regret having hurt someone I loved, and will always love, along the way.

{ 1 9 9 2 }

There is war in Bosnia, Rodney King in Los Angeles, Dan Quayle unable to spell potato in a New Jersey elementary school, and I spend the next ten long months filled with regret that I didn't eat more lasagna prior to starting my hideously grueling diet.

{1993}

The World Trade Center is bombed, Vaclav Havel is elected president of the Czech Republic, Heidi Fleiss is busted, and I deeply regret eating all that lasagna upon completion of my hideously grueling ten-month diet. There's an old saying: To consume one's own body weight in melted mozzarella is to go directly back to your fat pants.

{1994}

I don't remember much about that year except for this: The AIDS virus was savaging beautiful young men, and Mark Carson—my partner in crime, my in-case-of-emergency-please-call guy, my whip-smart, genuinely sweet, very brave, infuriatingly optimistic, darling friend—died as I held him in my arms. He had goodness, he had integrity, he had cheekbones that could open an envelope. He liked bright lights and big cities. He cared about justice and art. And in my dreams he's always there, dragging me to the best Turkish restaurant in Astoria or playing some CD of an obscure albeit amazing indie rocker, or simply racing forward to offer me sanctuary within his incredibly generous embrace.

I torment myself with regrets. They run the gamut from *I should have spent the extra money and bought a sofa that becomes a bed* to *I should have had more children*. What can I say? Fantasies fade, plans unravel, things change, and I grieve for the past as well as for Mark—as if the past were a fallen friend. But for all my coulda, woulda, shouldas, where Mark Carson is concerned my only regret is that we didn't get to grow old together. He'd have been dashing and I'd have been cranky, and together we'd have sipped green tea and watched old movies and catalog-shopped to our hearts' content.

Anyway, that's the ending I would have gone with if I were in charge of the planet. But I'm not even in charge of what to get on the pizza when I order takeout with my own child. About all any of us gets to be in charge of is who we are in our stories. In this story, I was keenly aware that Mark and I were on borrowed time, and it made me sit up and take notice of every bittersweet second. When time is of the essence, you get tickets to the show, you splurge on Christmas dinner and birthday presents, you stay up talking a little later, you pay attention. I memorized the clipped cadence of his voice and every expression that played across his gorgeous face. I watched as he gave and took, read and traveled, tried and failed, despaired and rallied, protested, partied, and persevered. And though he never found "the one," he loved and was loved in a world where love is sometimes pretty hard to come by.

There was an old woman I once knew who used to whisper this great thing whenever it was time to say goodbye; she'd pull you very close and, almost like a benediction, she'd murmur, "We only part to meet again."

What I wouldn't give to have that kind of faith. Oh, sweetie, how I wish I could pick up the phone and meet you for a cheeseburger at that very mediocre little diner on West Fifty-fifth Street, where I'd steal your French fries while you'd help me find a perfect note on which to end this chapter. But they turned that diner into a bank about three years back, which is just as well, as I could never walk in there without somebody asking where you were, until after a while, I couldn't walk in there at all. Life is joy and sorrow, hand in hand—you taught me that lesson nearly sixteen years ago. Today, the bank that was once a diner is now in free fall, we twitter and tweet, we look for doctors who will accept our insurance, provided we're lucky enough to have any. We still don't ask, and we still don't tell. We take stay-cations and go green and cherish our downtime and bail out the greedy and give till it hurts. We shoot for the stars, hope for the best, and brace for impact.

And life remains joy and sorrow. That's about the only thing I still know for certain. That, and this: I'll see you in my dreams.

11

THE HOURS

A FRIEND ONCE TOLD me about the Buddhist concept of pain without suffering; it's a notion that fascinates me. I mean, is it really possible to say, "Yep, my stomach aches, all right, but I don't have to add insult to injury by letting that pain run amok: I can skip the part where I moan, 'Now I can't meet my friends at the movie and I'll probably miss work tomorrow, which means I'll blow my deadline, lose my job, and die penniless and alone, never having seen *Indiana Jones Collects Social Security*'"?

Calming a frantic brain in the face of high anxiety is a pretty tall order, especially for a woman like me who tends to operate on two basic emotions: angst and barely suppressed angst. But assuming one can actually achieve pain without suffering, where else might this dynamic be applied? Is there such a thing as anger without brooding? Sex without strings? And the real question—my current obsession—can a person be unbelievably busy without being unbelievably overwhelmed?

Lately, I seem to have this constant sense that I'm just

keeping my head above water. I'm forever trying to catch up, stay in touch, and be where I'm supposed to be when I'm supposed to be there. I bought a new pair of jeans in November, but I've never worn them because I've never had a chance to get them hemmed. The last novel I remember curling up with is *Are You There God? It's Me, Margaret*—and that was in sixth grade. I floss while sorting mail, while defrosting lamb chops, while searching for Mrs. Weinstein, Julia's stuffed platypus. But this is not just about being a single mother (though I do spend an ungodly amount of time wondering why my daughter is not on a first-name basis with her stuffed platypus). Almost everybody I know— whether they're wealthy or struggling to make ends meet, whether they're bachelor girls or celebrating their twenty-fifth anniversary, whether their kids are grown or toddlers or nonexistent—*everyone* seems to be suffering from some sort of culturally induced A.D.D. Our brains are swamped and our bodies are tired. Blood pressures are up, serotonin levels are down, tempers are short, to-do lists are long, and nerves are shot.

Here's how I spent last Saturday . . . see if any of it rings a bell:

3:17 A.M. I am awakened by the sound of Julia's voice. "Mommy, Giovanni picked his nose and it bleeded," she informs me. "Good to know," I murmur. "Now go back to sleep before Mommy sends you to live in the lobby." Somewhere in England, the Supernanny is appalled.

4:26 A.M. I have to pee. My bladder used to be legendary. As God is my witness, I could go three, maybe four months without ever needing the ladies' room; I could drive from the redwood forest to the Gulf Stream waters sans bathroom break. But I'm forty-nine now and it's a whole new ball game.

4:27 A.M. I live in mortal fear that the slightest movement anywhere in the apartment will wake Princess Bunny Pie. I will not move. I will not move. I will not move.

4:33 A.M. I will move, but I will move in stealthy, gazellelike silence.

4:34 A.M. Here's the thing about stealthy, gazellelike silence—it's doable only if you don't step barefoot on a Lego.

5:19 A.M. Miss Cuckoo Pants insists it's time to rise and shine. I offer her a check for $260,000 if she will sleep for just one more hour. But the kid sees through me like a bar of used Neutrogena and reminds me that I still owe her eighty-five grand from the time she tasted a parsnip.

5:30 A.M. On goes the TV. The rule at this time of day is simple: She can watch anything she wants as long as it doesn't star Harvey Keitel . . . no *Bad Lieutenant*, no *Reservoir Dogs*, no *Taxi Driver*. You have to draw the line somewhere.

6:15 A.M. My little Goof Noodle is contemplative during her bath: "What are you thinking about, Jules?" "Mommy," she asks, "is Big Bird a boy or a girl?" I explain that we used to wonder the same thing about cousin Chris and that some answers are simply unknowable.

7:45 A.M. We have painted, we have Play-Dohed, we have read *Don't Let the Pigeon Drive the Bus* nine times in a row.

8:00 A.M. One of us is now wearing my lipstick, my jewelry, my sunglasses, my shoes, and two oven mitts.

8:30 A.M. I used to read the *New York Times*'s Arts & Leisure section and meet friends for scrambled eggs and a

Bloody Mary. Now I skim the Week in Review, toast a slice of low-glycemic Ezekiel bread, and follow it up with fifteen milligrams of Lipitor. Time is a thief.

10:00 A.M. The babysitter has arrived! I fully intend to have Lidra Basha babysit until the day Captain Monkey Toes leaves for college, at which point she can babysit me. For the record, I am well aware that there are women with more than one child and nobody to help them out, and if I could, I'd buy each and every one of them a single-malt scotch and a ridiculously expensive pedicure.

10:30 A.M. The trainer has arrived . . . or as I've come to think of him, Hitler in Nikes. After approximately fifteen minutes, I feel compelled to remind him that he has to marry me before he can actually collect on any life insurance policy. He ignores my plea for leniency, hands me two 15-pound weights, and tells me to "tighten my core." Where's Amnesty International when I need it, and for that matter, where is my core and when did it get saggy? One minute you and your boyfriend are finishing off a mushroom pizza with extra mozzarella, and the next minute you're realizing he didn't actually eat any. . .

12:00 P.M. I shower, change, and head for the supermarket, the dry cleaner, and the pharmacy, where I run smack into my evil neighbor. We are currently having a huge fight, but because I am not good at confrontation, she doesn't realize that we are having a huge fight and regales me with stories of her upcoming trip to Nepal. I glare at her and say in the iciest tone imaginable, "You, madam, are a gravy-sucking weasel, and I hope that you're forced to fly coach with an Ebola-riddled gibbon monkey stuck in your lap for sixteen straight hours." But because I am not good at deliberate bitch-iness, it comes out, "Great! Have a safe trip and let me know if you need someone to water your plants." Somewhere on the Upper West Side, a psychiatrist is cringing.

1:30 to 2:00 P.M. I miss my friends, so I try to hop off the hamster wheel and return a few calls. But Valerie has her daughter visiting from California, Brenda has her folks visit-ing from Detroit, Francesca is buried in paperwork, Mark is seeing clients, Jack and Sarah have four couples coming for dinner, Steffi has three weeks to find a new apartment, Peter is finishing his book proposal, Michael is in rehearsal, and Tori has set the day aside to "have a complete nervous breakdown." She assures me she'll be fine by 7:00, as she's got to get to Jack and Sarah's for dinner.

2:00 to 2:01 P.M. I take a minute to wonder why I wasn't invited to the dinner party and decide to be tremendously relieved.

2:02 to 3:30 P.M. I pay bills, fold laundry, write two thank-you notes for gifts I received last January, throw away everything that's gone furry or blue in my refrigerator, and wait for the nice man from Bloomingdale's to come and clean my filthy, horrible sofa.

4:00 P.M. The nice man from Bloomingdale's actually turns out to be a nice man. He tells me not to waste my money—cotton velvet isn't cleanable. The news hits me hard. I can roll with Afghanistan and a busted economy, but somehow the thought that cotton velvet doesn't clean well makes me want to crawl under the throw on my filthy, hor-rible sofa and never get up again.

4:02 P.M. I get up again. I am ghostwriting a book, and

four chapters are due by Wednesday morning. Clinical depression is not an option.

6:20 P.M. Suppertime. I cook wild salmon and broccoli for Colonel Cranky . . . assuming you define the word *cook* as "go to the little gourmet shop on First Avenue, buy and reheat." In any case, she will end up having spaghetti with butter and ketchup.

7:00 P.M. Before leaving, Lidra changes her clothes to go to a party. Did I mention that she's stunning? Did I mention that she's a size 0? Did I mention that I pulled a strand of ketchup-coated spaghetti out of my bra?

8:00 to 9:30 P.M. Sing "Head, Shoulders, Knees, and Toes." One of us is exhausted (it's that special kind of exhaustion that can only be achieved by singing "Head, Shoulders, Knees, and Toes" for an hour and a half) and would very much like to go to bed.

9:51 P.M. The three-book limit is imposed, and to my great relief, Senorita Knobby Knees dozes off without much protest. It's absurdly late, but because I don't get home from work until 7:00 each night, she doesn't want to go to bed at 8:15. Do I feel guilty? You bet I do.

10:00 P.M. to 12:30 A.M. A little more ghostwriting.

12:31 to 12:35 A.M. This is *my* time. I opt to spend it getting an MBA, forcing North Korea to stand down, curing cancer, and eating a small piece of cold chicken. Anyway, that's my plan, but knowing I have to water my evil neighbor's ficus tree tomorrow makes me skip straight to the barbecued chicken thigh and call it a night.

Sometimes I think pain without suffering, anger without brooding, being a parent, earning a living, maintaining friendships (hell, maintaining hair color), connecting with the universe, and dancing as fast as you can without screaming, "Stop the music; I want to sit this one out," just isn't an option for anybody anymore. We shoulder-roll out of bed in the morning and gulp coffee from Styrofoam cups on the way to wherever we're trying to go. We catch the sound bite, not the speech. We send the e-mail, not the love letter. We wait our entire lives to exhale. But I don't want to wait my whole life away. Nor do I want to wait until I retire fifteen years and eleven months from now . . . though I'm secretly hoping to develop one of those bubbly personalities that get you picked for *Deal or No Deal*, where I will win $400,000 dollars from Howie Mandel. We'll save for another chapter what it means that even in my fantasies I don't win the million . . .

My point is this: Spring is here! So this Saturday, I'm taking back my life or, at the very least, I'm taking a nap. If something's gotta give, it's not going to be me. I'm confining my work to regular business hours, forcing a friend out for coffee, reading for pleasure, bringing home daffodils, and eating a neon-pink marshmallow Peep with Miss Julia Claire Labusch. It's far from a solution, but it's a start.

$\mathcal{T}$HE SILENT KILLER

THE TERRORISTS ARE TERRIFYING, the glaciers are melting, and cancer has yet to be eradicated. So we wear ribbons and bracelets. We send money, guns, and lawyers. We raise awareness, we raise funds, we raise hopes. We are up to our earlobes in worthy causes. You show me a disease, and I'll show you a race for the cure. You see a natural disaster, I see Anderson Cooper in hip boots and a parka. Give me a calamity, and I'll give you a bipartisan commission issuing a report.

But nobody is out there tackling the really big issue. Yes, once again it falls on me to spearhead the campaign against a silent killer. It's insidious, it's crippling, and it plagues almost everyone I know. It attacks seemingly healthy males and females of all races and economic backgrounds, and though we may get better, precious few of us ever get completely well. I'm talking about the shame, the scourge, the heartbreak of *massive insecurity*.

Let's call it MI, because initials always sound more urgent when the celebrity spokesperson explains it to Larry King.

"Well, Larry," she'll begin tearfully, "my first bout of MI hit in seventh grade, right before Marcy Needleman's roller disco bat mitzvah party." Dabbing her smudgeproof-mascaraed eyes with a crumpled tissue, she'll take a deep breath and forge ahead. "How many nights have I lain awake asking myself the same question: Why, why, why did I choose that day to try parting my hair down the side?"

Before long I envision a "very special" episode of *Sesame Street*, in which Snuffy admits he suffers from MI and goes into rehab; a public service announcement encouraging teens to get tested before it's too late; and a magazine quiz zeroing in on the early-warning signs.

1. Before showing my upper arms in public, I first: (a) Make certain my tankini is clean and there's film in the camera. (b) Drink like there's no tomorrow and wait for a total eclipse of the sun.

2. I am being ignored by a snobby Beverly Hills salesperson. Therefore I: (a) Find the manager and explain that I am entitled to service and civility. (b) Slink away as if I had just been caught committing a felony or enjoying Scarlett Johansson's debut CD.

3. To secure the salary increase I want, need, and deserve, I meet with my boss and say: (a) I've taken on greater responsibility, and I believe I should receive greater monetary compensation. Here are several examples of the ways in which I've contributed to the quality of our product. (b) Um . . . I'm sorry, I'm

probably bothering you . . . in fact let me come back later, maybe . . . I just wanted to, um, say (*insanely long pause*), you're pretty.

4. I am on a first date with a very attractive man. I order: (a) Whatever I'm in the mood to eat. (b) A single grain of couscous because it's essential this person understand that I am dainty and delicate and exist on a simple diet of air and my own loveliness.

5. When I walk into a party where I don't see anyone I know, I think: (a) What a terrific opportunity to meet some new people! (b) I will spend the next nine minutes standing in the corner pretending to be onion dip, at which point I will fake a migraine, go home, put on my giant Detroit Tigers T-shirt, and watch a rerun of *Will & Grace*, the way God intended.

If you answered (b) to any of these questions, it is my sad duty to inform you that you could be one of the 6,576,344,362* members of society suffering from massive insecurity. (*Note: We do not include anyone who's been cryogenically frozen. Nor do we count one Howard J. Koppleman of Dayton, Ohio, whose parents inexplicably appear to have done everything exactly right—the entire Koppleman family is currently being studied by massively insecure researchers at NASA.)

What started this epidemic of insecurity? Maybe we were all left to cry it out in our cribs for too long, and it kept us from developing a healthy sense of entitlement. Or maybe we were held so much and hugged so close that it rendered us incapable of standing on our own two feet with any real confidence. Maybe we should blame our fathers (if for no other reason than it serves as a delightful change of pace from blaming our mothers), or maybe we should blame the solar system (I know I haven't been the same since they decided Pluto wasn't allowed to be a planet anymore), or maybe we should blame our gym teachers (dodgeball, anyone?), or maybe it doesn't matter who started it. What matters is that we don't seem to know our own worth. What matters is that we still worry the cool kids won't want to eat lunch at our table. What matters is that I have two different friends who wear makeup to bed because they're afraid to look like they actually look in front of the men they're attempting to dazzle.

So here are the choices: We could either hold a telethon to fight MI and perhaps raise enough money to get scientists started on a vaccine that will wipe the damn thing out once and for all; I mean, if we can destroy an entire layer of ozone in my lifetime, how hard can it be to get rid of our insecurities? Or we could decide to take a risk, say what we think, get up and dance, wear our crow's-feet like crinkly little badges of honor, acknowledge that it can be really, really scary to face the world head-on armed with nothing more than a strong sense of irony and a good pair of shoes—and then do it anyway. Me? Well, I'm hoping that vaccine is right around the corner.

$\mathscr{B}$ ED, BACON, AND BEYOND

I TEND TO BE a little whiny and, yes, it's been suggested, even a touch moody. Oh, I know what you're thinking: *You? But Lisa, you're so charming, so gosh darn delightful, so sparkly, so devil-may-care, so deliciously optimistic, so—what's the adjective—petite. It just seems impossible to believe that you don't actually rise and shine every morning ready to greet the world with that plucky, daisy-fresh, can-do attitude we've all come to know and worship. That is what you were thinking, right?*

The truth is, I get irritable. This was brought to my attention last summer when Johannes likened me to "Caligula with an earache." Now, in my defense, we were on an airplane with our squirmy daughter at the time, and, if memory serves, I had carefully dodged the drink cart and was making my way down the aisle with the aforementioned squirmy girl when we were trapped behind a guy who suddenly decided to store his trench coat in the overhead compartment as if he were part of the color guard folding the flag at Arlington National Cemetery.

In any case, I don't want to be the mean mommy. I don't

want to be the PMS-riddled girlfriend. I don't want to be the bitch in the house. So as I see it, there are three ways to achieve a little karmic retooling.

PLAN A: BUCK UP!
THINGS COULD BE SO MUCH WORSE

I have compiled a list of five key talking-myself-down points for those moments when it's so very tempting to complain bitterly, curse fate, or just plain mope.

- Does the word *Kabul* appear anywhere in my address?

- Is my postmilitary address a gurney at Walter Reed?

- Was I on the assembly line at General Motors?

- Am I trying to support my family on a minimum wage of $7.25 an hour?

- Did I somehow manage to get cancer without getting health insurance?

On the days I come home from the market only to realize I forgot the one item I actually went there to buy, I've decided that I will not scowl, I will not pout, I will not drop to my knees, shrieking, "Why, God, why," like when Sean Penn finds out his kid is dead in *Mystic River*. No, I will simply head back to the store secure in the knowledge that while I may occasionally forget the milk, I'm still able to remember the important conversations I have at work. And when you think about it, that puts me way ahead of every politician who's ever been called to testify before Congress.

PLAN B: GIVE IN!

THINGS COULD BE SO MUCH BETTER

According to a *60 Minutes* piece I watched (with the help of two glasses of a rather full-bodied Shiraz), our future is still being built on a deficit so gargantuan that it will have a cataclysmic effect for generations to come. To make matters worse, according to my cousin Rita, there isn't a decent pair of bone-colored espadrilles to be found in all of Westchester County. For those moments when it's so tremendously tempting to draw the blinds, mash the potatoes, and rent every mindless romantic comedy I was too embarrassed to see at the cineplex, I have written a permission slip to do that and more. A permission slip is a magical thing. It got me out of seventh-grade gym when I had my period, and it gets me out of grown-up life when I've had enough.

To Whom It May Concern:

Lisa Kogan is currently closed for repairs. She has been ridiculously wonderful for the last sixteen days in a row, and now she needs to eat bacon in her underwear. Please do not phone, e-mail, or make eye contact with her under any circumstances. You may approach only for purposes of foot massage (giving, not receiving) or to wonder aloud how she got so thin. Note to anyone currently sharing a home with Miss Kogan: In the event you happen to catch

on fire, be sure to drop and roll. Do not waste precious time
attempting to smother the flames by wrapping yourself in
a blanket, as the blankets will all be in use (and possibly
covered in a light dusting of bacon bits). As for any other
health crisis that might arise during Miss Kogan's time-
out: You will find Bactine in the bathroom, Band-Aids
in the pantry, and detailed instructions for giving yourself
the Heimlich maneuver under a Marge Simpson magnet
on the refrigerator door, just above the phone number for
the poison control hotline (which Johannes quietly posted the
first time he tasted her vegetarian chili).

PLAN C: FIGURE OUT
WHAT'S REALLY GOING ON

On my better days, I try to keep in mind that just as a rose
is not its thorns, a human being is not his or her cranki-
ness, and this realization generally serves me very well. I
only hope to God that the people I love will remember this
during my occasional cold snaps. If every once in a while I
get fed up, there's usually a reason. I guess for me the reason
isn't just that Johannes has described my coffee as "chewy"
or even that the French are no longer the only people in
the world who seem to hate our guts. No, I find that my
crabbiness factor skyrockets when I'm feeling overextended
and undervalued. Everybody wants to matter, and when we
think we don't, it's shockingly easy to retreat into misery
or impatience or sarcasm, or something else that's going to
make us hate ourselves in the morning.

A fine whine—no matter how momentarily satisfying—

leaves a helluva hangover. It curdles the heart and corrodes the world.

So I've decided to become unflappable. That's right, I'm taking a *Gray-skies-are-gonna-clear-up-put-on-a-happy-face* approach to life. Next time I get sneered at on the subway platform, or elbowed at a Starbucks, I will pretend I am starring in a 1940s musical. "*Golly,*" I will say to the moron who can't wait his or her turn, *you must be in an awful rush*! I will smile warmly. I will put out positive energy. If need be, I will summon a little empathy. I will try to understand what brings a person to a place where it becomes so easy to dehumanize his or her fellow human being. If it works, we will have a valuable exchange, a melding of the heart. If it doesn't, I will dump my Berry Chai Tazo Tea Infusion all over the creep, and run like hell straight back to my bacony little bed.

_T_HE FIRST BAD THING I EVER DID

How long have you and I known each other? Well, by my calculations we go back twelve or thirteen chapters now. This can mean only one thing: It's time for the monkey story.

There are those who will suggest that even to hint at the monkey story is to bring immeasurable shame upon the good Kogan name, that its mere mention invites the sort of familial acrimony and heartache seldom witnessed outside _King Lear._ Still, I will tell you the monkey story not because I want to—but because I must.

The monkey story takes place in the late 1960s. It was, as Simon & Garfunkel used to sing, a time of innocence, a time of confidences. I wore a "That Girl" flip and white vinyl go-go boots. Those boots were made for walking, so I'd walk two doors down the street to the Sapersteins' house because the Sapersteins had the biggest color TV on the block, and it was impossible to fully appreciate a masterpiece like _Batman_ in black-and-white. Anyway, at some point between Nixon's election and Elvis's comeback, my mother and father, brother and cousins all went to visit the grandparents in

Miami Beach . . . but not the Miami Beach you're thinking of. You see, before Miami was filled with fabulously sexy models eating fabulously sexy food at fabulously sexy boutique hotels, it was filled with old people who had dinner at 5:30 and worshipped Eleanor Roosevelt. As for entertainment, a kid could check out Ponce de Leon at the wax museum, play a rousing game of bingo, and still be bored silly by noon. And that, brings us to the monkey story.

There was (and I believe there probably still is) a place in Florida called the Monkey Jungle. It had funny little monkeys swinging from vines overhead, it had monkey memorabilia that made monkey memories last forever, it even had a monkey that was trained to put his hairy little arms around your neck and smile for the camera. I could go on, but suffice it to say the place was lousy with monkeys, and my cousin Suzie Gale and I thought we'd found paradise, complete with souvenir shop and snack bar. Then it happened.

Fact: Suzie was holding a peanut.

Fact: There, high above a large cage of spider monkeys, hung a gigantic sign that read DO NOT FEED THE MONKEYS.

Fact: I was always an inquisitive child, a sucker for an educational science project, if you will, and . . . hell, I wanted to know what would happen if I fed the monkey. Okay, strike that, I wanted to know what would happen if *somebody* fed the monkeys.

And there was sweet Suzie with her cherry-pink cheeks and her enormous angel eyes and her layers of dark, curly hair that rioted around that innocent freckled face, tangling and untangling according to the humidity, and, lo and behold, there was my peanut. "Suzie," I whispered with perfect non-chalance, "go see if that monkey wants the peanut."

Now, this next part happened rather quickly, and my recollection is a little hazy. If memory serves, Suzie walked over to the monkey cage and held the peanut up to the bars. The monkey took the peanut, and I could see Suzie beaming with pride as she turned to look at me. Unfortunately, I could also see the monkey toss the peanut over its shoulder, reach its menacing monkey paw between the bars, grab a chunk of Suzie's hair, and yank it out of her terrified little head.

I don't know how many of you have ever had to act as lookout while your mother crouches in a closet as she attempts to hide from her mother-in-law while phoning every pediatrician in the Greater Miami area to inquire about any potential issues that might arise "if, say, for example, your five-year-old niece happens to be mauled by a deranged monkey." Wait a minute, I do know. *None* of you have had to do that because I'm the only person in the universe who's ever sent her sweet little cousin out to be attacked by a monkey.

So that's the monkey story. It was the first bad thing I ever did—and I remember being shocked that Walter Cronkite didn't lead with it that night on the evening news. I guess Paul Simon knows his stuff—it really was a time of innocence. My family hadn't yet been touched by debt or divorce or death, and betrayal never amounted to more than a little bit of monkey business. The grown-ups smoked, the children tanned, we all ate red meat, and everybody thought they would live forever. But by the summer of '67, my hometown of Detroit was burning around us, and—thanks to James Earl Ray, Sirhan Sirhan, and a war we were assured was winnable—the shelf life on forever officially expired in the summer of 1968.

Suzie Gale eventually became Suzanne Rubini, an Atlanta attorney with a lovely husband, two terrific kids, and a fairly significant aversion to Curious George. Because my cousin is a charitable soul, and because she understood that I would do a much better job of beating myself up than she ever could, and mostly because her hair grew back, Suzie still speaks to me. Of course, these days the conversations tend to include a lot more about the cost of college than we ever would have imagined back when we played shuffleboard at our grandparents' condominium. And yes, the monkey story does occasionally come up, because it turns out you can't really have a monkey take a swipe at your head without mentioning it from time to time, but for the record, Suzie laughs when she tells the story. She's always been slightly sunnier than me—on a bad day, I can make Sylvia Plath look like a rodeo clown. And I've always been slightly funnier than Suzie—though she might argue that this is because I've never been attacked by a giant spider monkey. I still struggle with impulse control and guilt and the deeply unsettling truth that I am really quite capable of hurting the people I love; that, given the right set of circumstances, we all are.

Suzie and I are both a lot older and a little wiser now, and we've learned to pay close attention when a warning sign is posted right there in front of our eyes. We fasten our seat belts, we leave the tags on our mattresses, we refuse to operate heavy machinery after a tablespoon of Robitussin— and under no circumstances do we ever feed the monkeys.

ONE NIGHT ONLY

MINDY PERLMUTTER WAS HAVING a birthday party, but this was not just your garden-variety-chocolate-cake-two-kinds-of-ice-cream-balloons-and-a-piñata type soiree. No, this would be an affair to remember. This would be even more fabulous than Alicia Mittenthal's tie-dye-your-own-pillowcase gala or Daisy Feng's macrame-your-own-bracelet bash. This was to be a build-your-own-terrarium shindig, complete with colored sand and plastic stones and an incredibly classy assortment of glass goldfish bowls. At the time (the time being about thirty-four years ago), it seemed like a very big deal. I mean, let's be honest here, it would still be a big deal to go to a party where you get to build your own terrarium—in, you know, a kind of retro, '70s, ironic, hipster way.

So there I sat, looking out the den window, which gave me a clear view to the driveway while I waited for my ride to come spirit me away. Actually, it hadn't been our den since my grandparents returned from their life in Miami Beach and my folks rented a hospital bed to turn the den into my grandmother's bedroom. I loved my grandmother, but I can't say I ever really got to know her. She was the lady who played bingo and walked with a cane and kept a plump red tomato pincushion next to the creaky old foot-pedal-powered Singer sewing machine. I remember that she put up her own pickles and draped strudel dough across the kitchen table, and I know that she learned to reupholster her own furniture and got her first driver's license when she was deep into her fifties, and I'm acutely aware that she spoke to my grandfather in a very stern Yiddish whenever he tried to convince me to watch *The Lawrence Welk Show.* My grandmother endured an awful lot from the man, but no grandchild of hers was going to be forced to watch Lawrence Welk so long as she still had breath in her body.

Anyway, the sun was going down and my ride was running late and my grandmother started to talk. I thought she was going to warn me to be careful of something or other, because she was from the generation who believed that pigeons carry polio and she worried a lot, but if she was anxious about anything that night, she didn't show it. "I used to love to go to parties," she told me. She might as well have said that she used to enjoy scaling Mount Everest in flip-flops and a tutu. I was pretty sure I'd heard all the stories from my grandmother's life—and none of them involved a party.

The talk I'd heard was always the same: she and her mother and her five brothers and sisters starving through the bitter Russian winters in a little village whose name sounded like a sneeze. I knew about the malnutrition, the crippling rickets, the father who slaved away for years in Detroit trying to earn enough money to bring his wife and children to America and how when he finally did manage to save enough, the man he entrusted with the job of bringing the family over disappeared with the money (was he killed? did he steal it?), leaving my great-grandfather to start all over again. I'd heard how my great-uncles Sam and Isadore would scrounge through fields looking for anything edible while my grandmother supported everyone with her job as a maid to the butcher's wife, and I knew by heart the story of how she lost that job because the woman caught her taking a sip of milk. I also knew how she met Arthur Levi, the love of her life, who my great-aunt Molly swore looked "exactly like a young Perry Como," and that he died a few weeks after she married him, though she never stopped wearing his ring. I knew that the first son she had with my grandfather had died, and that on a Friday afternoon in 1938, her father, the man who worked so hard to bring the family here, died, too, after being robbed of the seven cents he had in his pocket and pushed off the roof of a building. And, of course, I knew that she worked nonstop to build a better life for her children.

But I realize now that I only knew those stories because they were told to me by other people. The night of Mindy Perlmutter's terrarium party, my grandmother was telling me the things *she* wanted me to know. She talked about dances and boys and a silvery blue dress she'd sewn with her sisters. She told me about a time when all her friends were doubled over with laughter because, well, I'm not really sure what it was they found so funny. There was a honk and the glare of headlights, so I gave my grandmother a fast peck on the cheek and flew straight out the door. She went into the hospital the next morning, and she never came out.

I sit playing Candy Land with the great-granddaughter Rose Kogan never got to meet. Julia Claire closes her eyes, blows on the dice, and whispers, "C'mon, c'mon, Mama needs a pair of deuces."

I have no idea why my six-year-old sounds like Edward G. Robinson, but I make a mental note to quit letting her play blackjack with the doormen. She rolls "snake eyes" and becomes my little girl again. "I want a do-over, Mommy."

I start to explain that we don't really get do-overs in this world, that you kind of have to play it as it lays. I believe the parenting books call this a "teachable moment," but my follow-through leaves much to be desired. I hand Jules the dice and say, "Go for it, kid."

The truth is, I want a do-over, too. I have ignored my instincts, I have embraced my neuroses, and there have been more than a few serious lapses in judgment over the years—hell, I once painted my bathroom aubergine. But if I could get just one night back, it would be a chilly October evening when nothing mattered more to me than hanging with my friends in Mindy Perlmutter's basement.

I would have taken off my coat and sat back down, only this time I'd have faced my grandmother instead of the driveway. I would have asked her if the good times outweighed the bad, if there were nights she'd do differently, if she'd ever felt like giving up—or if that was even an option. I never told her how smart and talented and brave and lovely I thought she was. I never heard what was so great about Greer Garson in *Mrs. Miniver*. I never found out what she did to make her skin so soft and her matzo balls so firm or if she'd have preferred it the other way around. And I never

thanked her for being my go-to grandma in the uncondi-
tional goodness department.

Julia and I finish the game and say our good nights. I am
eager to return a couple of phone calls, get her lunch packed
for school, and watch the episode of *Mad Men* I've got ready to
go on our DVR. But my daughter is feeling chatty. "Mommy,"
she begins, "do you know why the Princess Barbie Muske-
teers have swords that match their ball gowns?" Before I can
answer, she announces, "It's because they're royal squash-
bucklers." I tell her I'm pretty sure the word is *swashbucklers,*
and she tells me she's pretty sure I'm wrong and goes on talking. She doesn't want to let go of the night, and so I nudge
away two stuffed poodles and curl up beside her. The calls
and the lunch and even Don Draper can wait, because I have
learned the hard way that my job is to sit quietly in the dark
and listen to whatever my daughter has to say.

$\mathscr{T}$AKING A CHANCE ON LOVE

I BELIEVE IN LOVE. I believe it transforms, transports, and transcends. I believe it fine-tunes goodness, solidifies strength, ripens resolve, eradicates rage, alleviates stress, and elevates empathy. I believe in love (or something damn near like it) at first sight, I believe it's perfectly okay to love the one you're with, provided the one you're with either happens to have excellent news from an extremely up-to-date HIV test or answers to the name of Hugh Laurie, and I firmly believe that marriage ceremonies would go much faster if Kahlil Gibran hadn't written that big love passage into *The Prophet*. But more than anything else, I believe in love because when you don't have it, you tend to spend your every waking moment chasing after it . . . at least I always did. Bruce Springsteen was right—everybody has a hungry heart.

It's 10:00 P.M. and Johannes wants me to hang up the phone and help him fill out yet another private school application, in the sincere hope that Julia will be accepted by a good one and we can end our lives completely broke but secure in the knowledge that our kid didn't have to endure a 35-to-1 student-teacher ratio. He enters the room just in time to catch a snippet from my end of the conversation: "So does my friend absolutely have to love camping? I mean, what if she's perfect for you in every other respect—is the camping thing a deal breaker?" He rolls his eyes because he knows I'm on yet another in a long series of matchmaking missions. Technically, the camping thing is new on the checklist. Sometimes he gets to hear this: "And she has to be Jewish?" Sometimes it's something along the lines of: "His mother lives in Wisconsin, she won't be an issue." Or: "Look, I'll be honest, she could stand to drop ten pounds, but so could you." And then there's the ever popular: "I promise he's gorgeous . . . Of course, you might want to wear flats." Johannes listens for a minute, then performs a rather elaborate mime of making a noose and hanging himself as I lob a pillow at the side of his head and continue my phone call. "I know your last girlfriend forced you to sit through *Dialogues of the Carmelites*," I say patiently to the potential date on the other end of the line, "but this woman doesn't even like opera—I swear to you, she's completely uncouth." Johannes arranges his finger and thumb into a pretend gun, puts it to his left temple, and pulls the trigger. "Sorry, can you just hold on for one quick second?" I clamp my hand over the receiver and pose the question that crosses every woman's mind from time to time: "Why do you have to be such an idiot?" "Why do you have to set up everyone you meet?" he shoots back. "Because," I hiss through clenched teeth, "I want my friends to be as blissful as we are—goddamn it."

And the truth is, I do. There's no getting around it, couples fight. We all have that moment when it hits us that we've entered into a relationship knowing roughly as much about our soul mate as Mia Farrow did in *Rosemary's Baby*. Or, for that matter, as much as Mia Farrow did in her actual life. But I do like knowing that when I go to a black-tie affair clutching the satin evening bag that holds exactly one key and a pen, Johannes is the keeper of my Kleenex, lipstick, Tic-Tacs, and comb. I like knowing that once or twice a year he'll call me in the middle of the day to ask, "What don't I like again?" And I'll remind him that he can't stand cilantro, injustice, and the commercial where that talking fungus hides under the guy's toenail. I like knowing that if something happens to me, he'll be the one to decide if it's time to pull the plug. Sure, it's a little troubling that while shaving my legs the other day, I nicked my knee, only to look up and find him frantically searching for my living will—but Johannes has never been one to let things go until the last minute. Anyway, the point is, at the end of the day, it's good to have somebody. But finding that somebody is another story. That's where I come in.

MY 6 SIMPLE RULES
FOR SETTING UP FRIENDS

1. The Native Americans or the Arabs or the Japanese or some other highly evolved culture I can't think of and I'm too lazy to look up have this theory that every time you take a photograph of someone, you steal a bit of their spirit. I maintain that going on a bad blind date has that same effect. Try to keep that in mind. Avoid

phrases like "It's just a drink" or "It's only an hour out of your life." Those hours add up. Do not say, Hey, they're both single, so what the hell. Do your homework. Think long and hard about whether they're really compatible.

2. Think long and hard about whether they're really straight.

3. Keep expectations low. When describing the mystery suitor, it's best to avoid grand pronouncements à la "I've found you the man of your dreams!" Go with a light, casual "Well, he's originally from St. Louis and he has no visible nose hair."

4. You're going to be very tempted to try to find out if you made a love connection. Stop! Do not under any circumstances contact either party for postdate details. I mean it. Ditch your cell phone. Cancel your e-mail. If they had a good time, you'll hear about it.

5. Unfortunately, if they didn't have a good time, you'll hear about that, too. If one or both members of the date calls to say, "Your cousin Phyllis was all hands," or that your brother's former roommate spent thirty-eight minutes discussing the printer's credit at the bottom of the menu, you have but one choice: Fake a seizure. It's hard for people to complain if they think your airways are closing.

6. Remember that being single is not synonymous with being mentally impaired. So if your friends tell you there just wasn't any chemistry, trust them. Don't try to guilt them into another get-together; don't accuse them of being overly discriminating. It's sort of like what I did with Jules when she agreed to taste gefilte fish. You smile reassuringly, you say, "I'm proud of you for trying it," you remind her that "there are other fish in the sea," and then in the calmest voice possible, you add, "Please don't ever spit gefilte fish down the front of Mommy's blouse again." Your friend probably won't understand that last part, but it'll definitely take the conversation in a new direction.

You may wonder why so many of my rules deal with what to do when the date doesn't work out. Well, it's because true love is an incredibly elusive thing and, to be honest, most of the dates I fix people up on don't work out. Okay, *none* work out. But that doesn't mean it'll never happen. The day will come when my dental hygienist's niece and the guy who fixes my computer will meet for coffee, and coffee will turn into a movie, and a movie will turn into dinner, and if the stars are aligned and the gods are smiling, and nobody screws up royally, that dinner will turn into forever. Like I said, I believe in love.

${\mathscr K}$ OGAN'S HEROES

You COULD FILL ENTIRE football stadiums with all the things that I don't know. I don't know how to make paella. I don't know how to do algebra or iron pleats or ski. I don't know how to sing on key, accept a compliment, interact at a party consisting of more than eight people, or kill a lobster . . . which brings us back to my paella issues. But I do know a thing or two about men . . . okay, not two, but there is this one little thing about men that I do know with crystal clarity: I know what I like.

Needless to say, what I like, love, and cherish above all others is my own man. Johannes was a friend for quite a while, and then about seventeen years ago we went to a museum together and I stood there looking at a Giacometti sculpture through his faded denim gray eyes, and he was so funny, so astute, so sexy, so unpretentious that somewhere between the café and the gift shop, I was a goner. And (despite the fact that a mere twenty minutes ago we had an unbelievably irritating phone conversation) I still am.

But what if something were to happen to Johannes? I

mean, I realize that spending most of the year working in Switzerland isn't exactly on a par with spending most of the year working in Yemen, but things happen. Suppose he falls off an Alp or chokes on a chunk of chocolate? Do you have any idea how many human beings perish every single year in fondue-related accidents? Well, neither do I, but suffice it to say the statistics are probably off the charts. Anyway, forget Zurich: What if when Johannes is here in New York, he were to slip on one of the many, many wet towels he leaves lying all over the floor after his shower and then crash head-first into the guitar he has such a hard time pulling himself away from even though I'm late for work and could really use some help getting our daughter dressed (did I mention we had a big fight twenty minutes ago?), then who could I fall truly, madly, deeply in love with . . . after, you know, a suitable period of mourning? I've spent the last twenty minutes giving this matter considerable thought.

MEN I COULD FALL HARD FOR . . .
AFTER, YOU KNOW, A SUITABLE
PERIOD OF MOURNING.

- CEO/mensch Jim Sinegal came up with this utterly novel theory: If you hire good people and then treat them with respect, nice things happen. The nice thing is called Costco, a place where workers earn an average of $17 an hour and pay just 9 percent of their health insurance costs, a place that sells everything from Dom Pérignon to diapers at bargain prices. In a world where CEOs of billion-dollar companies require salaries to match, and wreck the economy in the process, Jim (as every employee calls him) takes home an annual salary of $350,000. I don't care if he's not a billionaire, Jim and I will live on love—and perhaps a 22-pound wheel of Jarlsberg cheese for the low, low price of $180. And when our days dwindle down to a precious few, we'll go online to the funeral department and get a terrific deal on matching, high-quality Costco caskets.

• Supremely skilled, deeply compassionate, cucumber cool, Andrei Rebarber, Daniel Saltzman, and Samuel Bender are the obstetricians who pulled me through a harrowing high-risk pregnancy. I'd like to take this moment to declare my undying love for these medical miracle workers and to offer a brief apology: Gentlemen, as you may be aware, the birth process is often a touch uncomfortable in an I'm-being-torn-limb-from-limb-by-a-horde-of-rabid-wildebeests-while-someone-sets-all-of-my-internal-organs-on-fire-and-stomps-up-and-down-on-my-tummy kind of way. It is possible that in the course of my twenty-two-hour labor I may have inadvertently referred to one or more of you as a motherfucking succubus . . . I see now that this was an unfortunate choice of words to use when requesting an epidural, and I am deeply sorry. It is further possible that you might have been bitten, kicked, pummeled, or clawed at in a manner that can best be described as "satanic." Again, I am beyond sorry. Finally, rest assured that I now fully understand that you were not in any position to prescribe heroin even if it were called for, and that any comments I might have made with regard to your manhood, your immediate family, or your innate sense of common decency were just terribly, terribly wrong.

- Some desire DiCaprio, others crave Clooney, I have a little thing for Desmond Tutu, or, as I like to call him, Archbishop McDreamy. What can I tell you? I've always been a sucker for integrity and twinkly eyes, which is why I'd also like to send a quick shout-out to Kris Kristofferson and Peter Falk.

- I never thought of myself as a particularly vain person; in fact I sort of prided myself on having a decidedly undiva-like attitude. But all that went out the window when I realized my face had to appear in the pages of *O* magazine every month. It turns out I'm ridiculously insecure and once lost an entire night's sleep worrying that my wrists looked puffy. Enter John Ritter. Not the late pratfall genius from *Three's Company*. No, the John Ritter I love illustrates my monthly magazine column. Here's a tip: If you're ever going to be viewed by millions of people on a regular basis, forget hair, makeup, and the South Beach diet—get yourself a man who sees grace where you can see only crow's-feet.

- After forty-nine Thanksgivings, I still can't make a decent turkey. Mine was so undercooked last year that several guests suggested a really good veterinarian could probably get it up and gobbling again. I love a man who can cook and I love a man who can write, and Anthony Bourdain is a man who can do both.

- I believe I could listen to Tom Waits singing "Take It With Me" every rainy Sunday for the rest of my life. I also love Johann Sebastian Bach, Ray Charles, Randy Newman, Bob Dylan, Stephen Sondheim, Johnny Cash, and the Beatles. They all make me happy and they all break my heart. And when you think about it, what else do you want from a musician?

- One hot summer night in the middle of the 1970s I sat in a 15,274-seat amphitheater just outside Detroit, Michigan, and watched a wild and crazy guy in a white suit perform "the disappearing dime trick." It was absurd and ironic, and exceedingly funny—it was the bravest act of comedy I'd ever witnessed. It was Steve Martin. He removed the arrow from his head a long, long time ago, but like comic geniuses from Buster Keaton to David Foster Wallace, he still performs a remarkable sleight of hand. Rent *Roxanne*, read *The Pleasure of My Company* or *Shopgirl* or a short story from his *Pure Drivel* collection called "Hissy Fit," and see for yourself how time after time, he manages to catch the pedestrian moment—the ordinary gesture—and wring it into an expression of exquisite longing. He was, is, and will always be my ideal combination of contemplative and cuckoo.

- Finally, there's the twentysomething model/actor/ Barneys clerk who sold me a pair of sunglasses I couldn't afford last Saturday morning. Shallow? You bet, but Desmond Tutu will only take a girl so far. I know Sunglasses Guy is an impossible fantasy, but you have to admit, he's a better option than Johann Sebastian Bach. Besides, I think there's something to be said for coming up with a list of impossible fantasies. Woman—at least this one—cannot live by reality alone.

Raise your hand if you remember that 1970s anthem "I Am Woman." For those of you who were too busy trying to grow out your horrible Jane Fonda-in-*Klute* shag to pay attention, the soaring declaration that made women all over America want to rally against injustice, macramé a belt, and stop serving beef Stroganoff at dinner parties went like this: "If I have to, I can do anything. I am strong! I am invincible! I am woman!"

My anthem would probably go, "If I have to, I can maybe do lunch. I am on Lexapro. I am responsible for Meredith, the class hamster! I am woman!" This is the kind of lyric that explains why I am so seldom called upon to produce a hit single, but we'll take a much closer look at that in my upcoming "What's Beyoncé Got That I Haven't Got?" chapter.

You now know the men I love and adore. Let's talk about a few good women.

I like women. I like them as much as or more than I like almost anybody. But the women I like best aren't always strong, and they're certainly not invincible. They're creative, they're idiosyncratic, and they're around if you need them. They complain, they console, and they can shop their way through virtually any crisis. They know how to raise hell and they know how to raise children. They can spot a scam, a lousy doctor, and a crummy boyfriend in under ten seconds. They've perfected the withering stare that makes a nasty salesperson, flight attendant, or co-worker fold like an origami swan. My favorite women may feel bad about their necks, but they feel pretty damn good about their legs. They do not trash their ex-husband's new squeeze monkey even if she happens to be eight months younger than their eldest daughter; they limit the amount of money spent sucking up to stepchildren; they try really hard to wish everyone well. They've never met a carbohydrate they didn't want to have a close personal relationship with. They brake for sex, sleep, and solitude, cashmere, caffeine, and Joan Didion. They've got nerves of steel, the courage of their convictions, and excellent footwear. They're sugar and spice and everything I aspire to. They remain cautiously optimistic.

Here, in no particular order, are a a few examples of the best and the brightest females I've come across.

She might have been born a coal miner's daughter, but Loretta Lynn raised herself up to be an audacious provocateur who's spent fifty years turning out serrated country classics like "Don't Come Home-A-Drinkin' (with Lovin' on Your Mind)," "The Pill," and "You Ain't Woman Enough (to Take My Man)." Her 2004 hit, *Van Lear Rose* (produced by White Stripes front man Jack White), came at age sixty-nine. When I'm sixty-nine, I plan to be watching reruns of

Who Wants to Be a Millionaire and obsessing over my cho-
lesterol . . . actually, that's pretty much what I'm doing at
forty-nine.

Long before those gorgeous Dove girls stripped down
for the camera, real women of every age, shape, and color
dressed up in this designer's easy, modern clothes. Eileen
Fisher seems to have invented Garanimals for grown-ups—
everything works with everything else and you don't need to
sell your bone marrow to buy a skirt. Were it not for my sister
Eileen, I'd be forced to walk around naked but for an old pair
of Doc Martens—and trust me, nobody wants that.

She understood female friendship, complicated men,
and domestic engineering better than most of us ever will.
I don't love Lucy, and I never dreamed of Jeannie—but
Wilma Flintstone could probably get us out of Iraq, end
global warming, and provide health care for all simultane-
ously. The question is this: Are we as a nation finally ready
for a cartoon cavewoman in the White House?

And, speaking of the White House, I'd like to thank
Chelsea Clinton for appearing to be a normal human being
when it would be oh so easy to go a different way. If anybody's earned the right to exit a limo without underpants,
lord knows it's her. There are no words for how grateful I
am not to have to watch as she checks out of rehab to attend
a Golden Globes party or serves forty-one minutes in prison
for shoplifting a leg of lamb in her Marc Jacobs bag or fights
for custody of the Octomom's septuplets or weighs in at
eighty-three pounds of solid denial. Bless you, Chelsea Clinton, for never presenting Victoria Beckham with anything
at the MTV Awards.

I know George Clooney isn't a woman, but I just saw a documentary called *Darfur Now* and it makes me like him so much that I've decided to bestow upon him an "Honorary Girl" title. He is self-deprecating, well informed, and fiercely committed to alleviating misery, so I say we hand him a DVD of *The Way We Were*, teach him the secret handshake, waive the membership fee, and start letting him into meetings.

"My faith in the Constitution is whole; it is complete; it is total. And I am not going to sit here and be an idle spectator to the diminution, the subversion, the destruction of [it]." The late, great congresswoman Barbara Jordan said that. I only wish other Texas politicians had shared the sentiment. I miss her. And I miss Ann Richards and Molly Ivins, too. I miss nobility and wit and idealism and style. I miss being the country that thinks torture is a really bad idea.

I met Jan Frank in kindergarten more than forty-four years ago. We starred in the Fred D. Leonhard Elementary School production of *The Wizard of Oz*, she as the Wicked Witch of the West, me as Dorothy . . . okay, fine, Suzie Daitch was Dorothy, I was Winkie Girl Number Seven, and for those of you playing the home game, that's a notch below Munchkin . . . not that I'm bitter. We read Judy Blume, we survived our bat mitzvahs and driver's ed (which went better once Jan was able to stop shrieking long enough to take the wheel from me), we broke up with boyfriends, buried our grandparents, raged at our mothers, erupted in geysers of emotion, got our teeth fixed and our complexions under control. I was the maid of honor at her wedding and she was at the hospital before my daughter was six hours old.

As I sit typing away on this rainy Monday afternoon, Jan, my oldest friend on earth, is at a different hospital. Right about now, she is having a rare form of sarcoma cut out of the area just beneath her left collarbone. I wish that I were with her, but she's got the world's best husband for that particular assignment and so I do what I know how to do . . . I wait patiently, worry endlessly, and pray to a God whose existence I doubt regularly. I'm tired and pissed off today because it's pouring and because Jan has three magnificent boys at home and because this should not be happening to my favorite confidante. But then I remind myself that if we have to, we can do anything. We are strong, and when one of us isn't feeling all that invincible, the other will always take the wheel. We are women.

*T*O GRANDMOTHER'S HOUSE WE GO

HERE IS A BRIEF list of the people who have served me well: Catherine de Medici, who at some point around 1533 came down heavily in favor of the fork, giving it some degree of social acceptance (without Cate I'd be forced to treat spaghetti Bolognese as finger food); Dr. Earle Haas, who, bless his heart, on November 19, 1931, filed the first patent for a tampon (I think of him fondly every time I start to bloat, break out, or cramp); and one Mr. Erik Oley, who, on July 23 of this very year, turned to me and uttered a sentence that would forever change my life: "Lisa," he said, "when we travel with the kids, we use a rechargeable battery that keeps the portable DVD player running an extra six hours." Yes, the fork is handy, the tampon miraculous, but thanks to friend, humanitarian, and potential saint Erik Oley, Julia is now able to enter an airplane in New York and exit it in Switzerland having seen every *Charlie and Lola* cartoon ever made. Twice.

Traveling the world is romantic, exhilarating, life changing— and just not my thing. When I was young and carefree, I hitchhiked through Nepal . . . okay, I was never young and carefree—I was the seven-year-old yelling at the other kids to quit throwing stuff before they put someone's eye out, and, if you must know, it was actually my friend Adele who hiked through Nepal. I would have gone, but every time I weighed snowcapped mountains against toasted English muffins and a pedicure, questing for a backpack full of experience always finished second. It isn't that I don't sometimes gaze up at the moon and dream of touring every planet in the solar system, but who are we kidding? I can't make it to the dry cleaner before he closes, so getting myself to the moon seems like a real long shot. These days when I'm in the mood to observe a bleak, dust-covered terrain with virtually no detectable signs of life, I mix up a tall glass of Tang and check out my bedroom.

Given this overwhelming desire of mine to remain swaddled in a queen-size duvet eating Jell-O sugar-free chocolate pudding for the rest of my natural days, it is one of life's great ironies that I hooked up with a guy who lives on another continent.

The holidays are upon us, and unfortunately over the river and through the woods to Grandmother's house we go is only doable if your grandmother happens to be conveniently located over the river and through the woods. Julia's grandma lives in a small German village, a place where everything—fruit, vegetables, fish, gingerbread, marzipan, strudel, small children, churches from the fourteenth century, cobblestone streets, Volkswagens, you name it—is drenched in some sort of cream sauce, and it is literally impossible to get even a single ice cube for

the Diet Coke you are drinking in a futile effort to miti-
gate the effects of all that heavy cream. The truth is, I
wouldn't want to live there, but it really is a nice place to
visit. It's the place where I have the luxury of reading long
books and running around without my watch and sipping
tea every afternoon. It's the place where I get to see Julia
pluck grapes and strawberries right off the vine and pop
them into her mouth. The place we go to water pale peach
dahlia blossoms in the back garden or pick plums from the
tree in the front yard and hang around the kitchen as her
grandmother bakes them into a tart (topped, of course,
with heavy cream). I lucked out in the mother-in-law department; Ulrike and I get on well together. But I believe
the secret to our success is probably that she speaks very
little English and the only word of German I know is *dachs-
hund*. Our conversations usually go like this:

Ulrike *(big smile)*: You like some schwimflugels mit your
   knoblauch?
Me *(big smile)*: The horse rides at midnight.
Ulrike *(big smile)*: Shmetterlink sweeten the gloffgarten.
Me *(big smile)*: Jack Spratt could eat no fat.
Ulrike *(big smile)*: Johannes, komm rein!
Me *(big smile)*: Johannes, get in here!

Where my parents might take us for Chinese food and
bowling, Grandma Ulrike takes us into the forest to feed
corn kernels to the wild boars. Where my parents might
switch on a Wiggles CD, Grandma Ulrike is strictly Bach.
In my folks' gated community, we swim at a chlorinated

pool. In Germany there is a lake. And Julia, who is a proud graduate of the International Preschool at the United Nations, loves it all. I envy her freewheeling spirit, her ability to roll with the punches of severe jet lag, her delight in packing a bag ("Jingly ball. Check. Paper clip. Check. Grasshopper finger puppet. Check. Okay, I'm ready!") and taking off for parts unknown. I hope at some point to be as secure in the world as my little girl is. I hope wanderlust can be cultivated. I hope one of these days I'll learn to relinquish control, skepticism, and all the fears that keep me grounded. I hope the journey becomes every bit as lovely as the destination. And beyond all of that, I hope one day to be thin enough that I can actually afford to down a summer vacation's worth of cream sauce.

*U*P ON THE ROOF

HERE IS MY NEW Year's Rockin' Eve fantasy: a lipstick-red strapless dress (think Ava Gardner in *One Touch of Venus*) finished with a pair of Brian Atwood heels that make your legs look like the floor is the only thing that's stopping them from going on forever, a crystal flute of Veuve Clicquot, a little *Auld Lang Syne*, a lot of colored lights, and the man of your dreams (obviously, in this case, that would be Johannes—not Jonathan Rhys-Meyers, not Jeffrey Dean Morgan, not the green-eyed guy who sold me sunglasses at Barneys—and shame on you for dragging them into this) takes your face in his cool, confident hands and gives you the kind of kiss that makes the world fall away just as the clock strikes twelve. Friends are giddy, caviar is glistening, the old year is ending, and the new year is whatever I say it is.

Here is the reality: Ava Gardner put on a housecoat the minute the director yelled "Cut," caviar makes my ankles swell, and New Year's Eve has never once lived up to its billing. I spent eighteen years in a tiny studio apartment just a few short blocks from Times Square, and I'm here to tell you

I saw things—ugly, hard-partying, throw-uppy things—
that never made it onto any Dick Clark special. I mean, I like
a disco ball and confetti as much as the next girl, but there's
something about forced frivolity that feels so, well . . .
forced. Then, a few years ago, I took a radical step: I quit.
You heard me: I dropped out of New Year's Eve. I mailed
my formal letter of resignation to Ryan Seacrest, explaining that the urge to go out and get crazy has been replaced
by the urge to stay in and get sane (or a reasonable facsimile
thereof). I said, "So long, sucker," and I never looked back.

Here's the routine I employed in the early days of my gala-
free existence. I'd slip into something a little more comfortable (we're talking Detroit Red Wings jersey and tube
socks). I'd cook a lovely meal and eat it at a table set so perfectly it would make Colin Cowie weep. I'd rent anything
with Katharine Hepburn—*The Philadelphia Story, Bringing Up
Baby* (hey, if Cary Grant happens to show up, so much the
better)—and then—drumroll, please—I'd pick my worst
set of drawers, my messiest closet, my highest mountain of
old papers, and start chipping away at the chaos that had
given me grief all year long. I was ruthless in my pursuit of
clarity: dog-eared Crate & Barrel catalog from last spring,
gone! Thomas Friedman article I meant to copy for everyone I'd ever met, out! The *New Yorker* with that incredible
Art Spiegelman cover, bye-bye, baby—it was great fun, but
it was just one of those things. My friends would wake up
with hangovers while I would wake up with a clean closet
and at least half a dozen bags of stuff for Goodwill. I felt
calm, I felt virtuous, I felt really, really out of it.

Then one fine day, Johannes went from friend to boyfriend-with-son, and Jules came along, and suddenly the lovely meal I'd always prepared was replaced by a hot dog for Julia, fish sticks for Jonathan, who doesn't eat meat, and finally, at that inevitable moment when Jules gets cranky and begins pelting Jonathan with his own fish sticks and Jonathan can't be in the vicinity of a nonvegetarian hot dog without making obnoxious gagging sounds, I'd go to plan B: macaroni and cheese for all. The Katharine Hepburn movie gave way to a Hannah Montana video, and the messes that used to drive me nuts stopped getting to me in quite the same way. I finally figured out that life is inherently messy and it takes a lot more than a New Year's Eve purge to bring it under control.

So now, when December 31 rolls around, I abdicate control. I invite two or three close friends to stop by if they're so inclined; and if they're not, Johannes and I like to devote at least a couple of hours to horrifying the children with our general dorkiness. Last year, just before midnight, we got ourselves and the kids all bundled up and headed to the roof to watch fireworks light up the East River. We were pleasantly surprised to discover that unlike the Fourth of July, we had the entire roof all to ourselves. It was around 12:03 P.M. when one of us remembered that there are no fireworks over the East River on New Year's Eve.

I guess sometimes you just don't get fireworks. But every once in a while, you get something even better: We stood there, huddled together at the top of the world in our flannel pajamas, down jackets, mittens, and scarves, our breath coming out in soft puffs that mingled and hung in the night, laughing like fools—thinking that for better or for worse, these are the good old days.

$\mathscr{L}$ OVE, LOSS, AND WHAT I ATE

I JUST FINISHED READING *Love, Loss, and What I Wore* for the 219th time. It's a quirky little autobiography in which the utterly charming Ilene Beckerman recalls her life's defining moments through the wardrobe choices she's made—from Brownie uniform to bridal veil.

The book got me digging through my own closet full of milestones, but clothes have never really been my thing, so here is all I can report from the fashion front: When I was five, my parents took me to see *Snow White*. I have a clear memory of wearing a sleeveless orange sundress dotted with little white flowers and thinking that when I grew up I would do whatever it took to avoid a gig where I had to be the cleaning lady for a houseful of diamond-mining dwarfs or, for that matter, any man who goes by the name of Sneezy. I also have a clear memory of being thirteen and getting the perfect dress for Michael Lasky's bar mitzvah. Unfortunately, Judy Glassman got the same perfect dress and Judy Glassman was adorable. Thanks to 308 years of rigorous psychotherapy, I'm now almost able to believe that

I, too, was adorable, but not even Paul McCartney himself could've convinced me of that back in the day. Finally, I will admit that somewhere between 1961 and this morning there appears to have been a fake fur vest, a pair of pink pleather hot pants, and something that, were I feeling really, really charitable, could best be described as a staggeringly festive sombrero . . . with antlers.

And that pretty much sums up the last forty-nine years of my life in clothes. Believe me, Beckerman did it better— my story just doesn't quite work when filtered through the prism of ball gowns and bathing suits because, frankly, even if I were the Belle of the Ball or the Bunny of the Beach, it isn't the stuff I wore that stays with me.

- The first time I visited France, I did not sleep on the eight-hour flight for a perfectly reasonable reason; I wanted to be preternaturally alert in case the pilot suddenly needed me to land the plane. You may be wondering why he wouldn't simply turn to his or her co-pilot for assistance. I don't know. You may be wondering if in fact I have a pilot's license. I do not. You may be wondering how many other delusions of grandeur I currently suffer from. Dozens. My point is that the first time I saw Paris—it was through profoundly jet-lagged eyes.

- Here's everything I know about French cooking: (1) Julia Child was a genius and (2) those little rodents in that *Ratatouille* movie could not have been more darling. As for what I know of the French language, well, suffice it to say that I once walked into a small pharmacy just outside Lyon and tried to buy a tube of "KY marmalade." Want to know what you get when you combine a distinct lack of foreign language skills with a limited knowledge of haute cuisine and a dash of sleep deprivation? You get a plate of scandalously rare meat with a raw egg perched on top. You also get me screeching across the rather sedate Parisian bistro, "Holy shit, there's an *oeuf* on my *boeuf*!"

• As a show of solidarity with my first true love, I once went on a hunger strike. I forget what our cause was but in my heart, I'm sure it was relevant and meaningful and exactly the kind of thing Pete Seeger would want to get behind. Anyway, about four hours and forty minutes into our strike, the boy met a platinum blonde who looked a little like Judy Jetson and I devoured a toasted sesame seed bagel with cream cheese and chives. Note, that out of respect for history's great hunger strikers, Mahatma Gandhi, Cesar Chavez, Alice Paul, I steadfastly refused my mother's many offers of a little smoked whitefish to go with the bagel.

• Upon breaking up with my next first true love, a delightful young gentleman whom many of my friends still affectionately refer to as "evil incarnate," I invented the ultimate my-boyfriend-has-just-dumped-me food. Prehistoric man came up with the wheel, Steve Jobs created the iPod, but let the record show that it was I who brought the world the dessert potato. Yes, the dessert potato, because nothing says "I'm hurting" quite like a woman who hasn't showered in nine days chowing down on an eleven-ounce Yukon Gold that's been slathered in sprinkles and marshmallow fluff while the greatest hits of Janis Ian play on in an endless loop of sheer misery.

• I like my pizza like I like my men: hot, no-nonsense, and covered in melted cheese. And though I've never been especially religious (this despite having once seen a yam that was a dead ringer for Golda Meir), I'm telling you that as transcendent experiences go, it's pretty hard to beat Buddy's Pizza in Detroit, Michigan. I could rhapsodize about the pure perfection that is Buddy's pillowy yet crackly crust with its ever so slightly fried edges and almost golden center. I could gush endlessly over the harmonic convergence of sauce and mozzarella, the hint of garlic and oregano, the touch of provolone, but for reasons that will never be entirely clear my editor has refused to provide the twenty-nine extra pages I requested. Just know this: Despite everybody saying that when the country gets a cold, Detroit goes straight to bed with the flu, that it's got the highest unemployment rate, the most messed-up housing market, that the last one out should be sure to turn off the lights, I still believe in the Red Wings, the auto workers, and Smokey Robinson. I had Buddy's Pizza on my first date, I had it at my sweet sixteen, I had it the night before I moved to New York City, I have it every time I come home, and I can assure you that where there is Buddy's, there is hope.

- My first Halloween as a full-blown adult! Because I did not live in a residential neighborhood, I expected no more than five or ten kids to ring the bell of my tiny studio apartment, but I had failed to take the divorced dad contingency into account, so faster than you can say "Disney Princess," I was picked clean by an unruly mob of trick-or-treaters. By 8:15 I found myself handing out beef bouillon cubes and instructing a dozen toddlers all hopped up on Hershey's kisses and candy corn to "just add boiling water and give it a stir." This is when it first occurred to me that being a grown-up on Halloween, or on any of the other 364 days every year, is actually much, much harder than it looks.

- It's early in my relationship with Johannes. He loves roast chicken, I love him and love, as we all know, makes normally reasonable people into low-grade lunatics who think nothing of pickling their own peaches, freezing homemade pesto, and buying special molds that make little heart-shaped ice cubes. These days I'm generally unwilling to walk across the room to get Johannes a fork but there was a time when I would have happily made my own water from scratch if he so much as glanced in the general direction of a faucet.

  The plan is simple: I will enter the kitchen on a Thursday morning with garlic, lemon, tarragon, kosher salt, thyme, rosemary, and half a dozen organic chickens. I will not reemerge until I have perfected the art of roasting a chicken. Nearly nine hours later, I have brined, I have trussed, I have tented, I have basted, I have filled cavities with pierced lemons, I have slipped herbs beneath skin, I have contaminated cutting boards and let juices run clear. I have cursed in ways seldom heard outside of maximum security prisons, maternity wards, and HBO. I have spent an inordinate amount of time and energy thinking about how lucky dead people are. I am drenched in sweat and coated in chicken fat, but I've done it! I've mastered roast chicken for the man I love. The meat is moist, the skin is crispy, the seasoning is sublime and all's right with the world.

A week or so later, our neighbors Nick and Diane invite us upstairs for an impromptu dinner. Not only is her chicken spectacular, somehow she has managed to look as if it won't be necessary to have her institutionalized. "They roast them on a spit at that new supermarket across the street," she explains. "They're only $6.95 and I've never tasted better roast chicken in my life," Nick says, reaching for a drumstick. Johannes stops licking his fingers long enough to add, "Neither have I."

In every relationship, there comes that special moment—that very first time you kick your partner under the table and follow it up with a quiet albeit menacing glare that says, "I could crush your windpipe using only my thumb and forefinger." It wasn't rational and it certainly wasn't right—but this was our moment.

- I have a food processor that slices and dices, shreds and minces like nobody's business. But it seldom sees the light of day, because I have this other gadget, an ancient hand chopper consisting of two curved metal blades attached to an ordinary handle; also attached are some of the loveliest memories I own.

We are standing in my mother's kitchen. We are both a little eccentric, a little complicated—my grandmother and me. I am five, and she is seventy, or I am thirty-one and she is ninety-six, it doesn't matter, the ritual remains unchanged: Into the biggest wooden bowl I've ever seen go whatever peppers, red and green, can be found in the fridge. Carrots and parsnips are peeled and tossed in, too, along with celery stalks, potatoes, tomatoes, onions, and the odd bulb of fennel. Next my grandmother takes hold of the chopper that her mother and very possibly her mother's mother once used, and begins the serious work of bouncing the blades up and down till the bowl is filled with chunks and cubes and a green, earthy fragrance. Now it's my turn. The paint on the handle may be chipped, but the blades are as sharp as ever. I rock them back and forth until a bright confetti of fresh vegetables is ready to be added to the beef bones simmering on the stove.

We made this soup a hundred times, but I can't recall a single conversation we had while we did it. I know she taught me to clean up as I go along. I know she believed it was sinful to waste even a scrap of food, "Ruthie Rothman throws half the apple away with the," she would complain in a tone usually reserved for Nazis and Nixon. I know she ached for her mother till the day she died. And I know that one day my daughter will learn to make soup with an old-fashioned, handheld chopper that's missing just a little bit of paint from its antique handle.

*Y*ESTERDAY, WHEN I WAS YOUNG

I HAD IT ALL down to a system. Whenever a conversation would turn to the subject of age, I'd casually mention that I was twenty-eight, or thirty-seven, or forty-two, or however old I was at the time and then I'd pause, magnanimously allowing people the beat they needed to acknowledge their surprise and commence with their compliments. "You're kidding," they'd gush. "I mean you sure don't look [fill in the blank] years of age." This is where I'd generally blush slightly and mumble something just a touch self-deprecating about how God probably figured giving me split ends was enough. But I was being coy, and we both knew it. The truth is, I have never looked my age.

Then something happened. While chatting with one of the other mothers at my daughter's school, I casually mentioned that I'm about to turn forty-nine and, naturally, stood back, waiting as usual for the shock and awe to set in. Only it didn't. Perhaps she was distracted. Perhaps she didn't hear. "Yep," I went on, "the big four-nine . . . can you believe it?" She didn't appear to have any trouble believing it. I searched for an explanation: Isn't this the same mommy who forgot the class snack? Didn't she inadvertently kill her kid's radish-plant-in-a-Dixie-cup project? Perhaps she's a teeny bit deranged, I reasoned, and wrote the whole thing off as an isolated incident.

Only it wasn't. Over the next few weeks, it happened again and again . . . and again. My date of birth came as no surprise to the new dentist. The woman who renewed my passport didn't give it a second thought. My mother actually changed the subject. Soon I began desperately shoehorning my age into even the most mundane exchanges, hoping against hope that I would once again hear all about how young I look. Only I didn't.

THE BUTCHER: Should I bone the chicken breasts?

ME: You know, I'm not exactly a spring chicken myself.

THE BUTCHER: (*Odd grunting sound coupled with cold, dead, heartless stare.*)

ME: I mean I'm practically forty-nine . . . can you believe it?

THE BUTCHER: I'm leaving the bone.

ME: My grandma always looked good for her age, so I guess . . .

THE BUTCHER: Next.

There comes a moment when you know that your face has changed; when that effortless glow you always had going for you suddenly requires major effort. For me, that moment came on the fifth of August at 4:13 P.M., eastern daylight

time, while buying a pound and a half of chicken breasts at
Golstein & Sons.

The thing about being young, or at the very least, looking
young, is that you honestly think you'll live forever. And the
thing about not being young is that it finally dawns on you
that you won't. I stare into the bathroom mirror as my fingertip traces a line in my forehead that I swear wasn't there
yesterday, and just as sure as I know I was born, I now know
that one of these days I'm going to die.

It saddens me that unlike Leona Helmsley, I do not have
a yappy little Maltese dog to whom I can bequeath my vast
fortune. It further saddens me that unlike Leona Helmsley,
I do not have a vast fortune. Still, I've got stuff . . . not good
stuff, not giant-flat-screen-TV, fabulous-shoe-collection,
secret-family-recipe, antique-emerald-brooch stuff, but stuff
just the same. So without further ado, here is my last will
and testament, or as George Carlin used to say, "a place for
my stuff."

I know there are many who choose to donate their bodies
to science, and may I just say what a noble choice that is.
But I have yet to forgive science for forcing me to dissect
a frog in seventh grade—like I didn't have enough to deal
with as a preteen geek in Southfield, Michigan—so in the
unlikely event that he doesn't already have it at the time of
my passing, I want to donate my body to Mr. Benicio Del
Toro, because, let's face it, if he can't bring me back to life,
nothing can.

I think my long-suffering assistant, Polly Brewster, would
agree that I became a much better boss right around the time
she repeatedly began asking if I'd seen *The Devil Wears Prada*.

But as I look over at Polly proofreading one of the 17,000 essays I've written to get my daughter into a decent school, I realize it'll take more than a Banana Republic gift certificate at Christmas to secure a permanent place in her heart. So, Polly, I offer you all the office supplies (including but not limited to stapler, tape dispenser, Post-it notes) you can get your hands on before somebody points out that they belong to the Hearst Corporation.

I remind my old friend Brenda Josephs of our Sunny von Bülow pact: If ever I end up in some kind of irreversible coma, I fully expect you to come by every few weeks and pluck any unsightly facial hair that might spring up. I'll be surrounded by doctors, so for God's sake, Brenda, throw a little lip gloss on me and, by all means, help yourself to my Partridge Family albums.

I would like to leave Johannes Labusch (the light of my life, the low-fat vanilla yogurt of my blueberry parfait) the freedom to remarry after I'm gone. I'd like to do that, but technically, my love, you never did marry me. A minor detail, really. You go right ahead and tie the knot with my replacement, buy that ring, rent that tuxedo, introduce your great-aunt Elfie to your brand-new in-laws. I'm certain that if your fiancée has got the taste and judgment to pick you, she'll make an excellent wife and loving stepmother. I have but one request: Do not under any circumstance have sex with this tramp. Or if you must, let it be with the under-standing that—and I say this in the most tender way imag-inable—I will poltergeist you to a degree that makes *The Amityville Horror* look like *The Sound of Music*.

Last but never ever least, I leave my lovely and amazing

daughter, Julia Claire Labusch, and the most beautiful boy on earth, Julia's half brother, Jonathan Anteo Labusch, the comfort of shared experience and unwavering friendship, because honestly, that's just about the only defense against the world's darkness that I know of. So, Julia, you get Jonathan, Jonathan, you get Jules, and as long as I'm on a giving streak, you guys both get my favorite quote from the book we were reading last night when one of us (okay, me) fell sound asleep. I'm hoping that if you don't quite trust me on this, you'll consider taking Christopher Robin's word for it just the way that Pooh did: "You must remember this: You're braver than you believe, and stronger than you seem, and smarter than you think." And, if you'll permit me one final piece of advice: See if there's any way you can make friends with Leona Helmsley's Maltese.

*H*OW YOU (YES, YOU!) SHOULD
LIVE YOUR LIFE

IN 1977, MY FRIEND Brenda and I went for dinner at a little Chinese restaurant called Empress Garden. She had the lemon chicken, I had the shrimp har kow, and we each had an egg roll because in 1977 you could eat sugar and fat and deep-fried everything without its signifying that the apocalypse was at hand. Our waiter placed the entrées in front of us and ceremoniously lifted the shiny silver domes. Brenda's chicken was crunchy on the outside, moist on the inside, lemony all over, and I knew in an instant that I'd made a hideous error in judgment—I should've gone with the chicken.

I tell you this story to illustrate my willingness to admit when I've made a mistake. In fact, I've rarely ordered a breakfast, lunch, or dinner I didn't regret; at this very moment I'm wishing I had an iced tea instead of a Diet Coke. But aside from the food thing and one very cute guy in the early '80s who was all you'd want in a man except for the fact that he was also looking for all you'd want in a man, I am never, ever wrong.

———

Now, I'm not saying I always take my own advice or trust my own instincts. I'm merely suggesting that the world would be a much better place if everyone else were to do exactly what I tell them to do. Arrogant? You bet. Narcissistic? I suppose. But c'mon, admit it, you've had the very same thought kicking around for years. Still, I'm the one with the book—so now without further ado . . .

EVERYTHING I KNOW ABOUT THE WORLD AND HOW YOU (YES, YOU!) SHOULD LIVE YOUR LIFE

• If you can't get a babysitter, for the love of God, stay home! I don't want to be sitting next to little Charlotte and Duncan as they fight over a Raisinet at the midnight screening of the Lars von Trier film festival. You wanted kids, so suck it up, walk it off, subscribe to Netflix.

• If your outgoing phone message is longer than, let's say, the Jean Hersholt Humanitarian of the Year segment of the Oscars, it's time to rerecord.

• Calling to let your friend know you're running late does not excuse your constantly running late.

• I'd like to say something to every crabby airline passenger who responds with disgust whenever a baby cries. Perhaps you don't know how babies work, but there's been a study, and it turns out that giving a four-month-old the stink eye doesn't actually accomplish anything. Either have a little compassion or have a little Ambien.

• One word: Floss.

• Any man who begins a conversation with "I don't want to hurt your feelings . . ." is about to hurt your feelings. It's the kind of phrase that's never followed by "but I just don't think you're eating enough. Please have more French fries while I go get you a brownie." Other opening gambits that pretty much scream duck-and-cover include: "Don't take this the wrong way . . . ," "You can feel free to say no . . . ," and the always popular "Look . . ."

• Enough with celebrity gossip. The problems of Lindsey Lohan should not be competing for the headline space in our brains. We have to be smarter than that, and if we're not, we have to pretend that we are.

• Get so excellent at something (long division, friendship, Parcheesi, removing cranberry juice stains, découpage—it doesn't matter what) that your genius will be impossible to ignore and your legendary expertise at removing cranberry juice stains while dividing six-digit numbers by thirty-seven will either bring you glory beyond your wildest dreams or, at the very least, help you feel vaguely competent as you make your way through the world.

- Allow me to demystify the entire real estate market for you. *Gracious* means insanely small. *Quaint* means a godforsaken wreck and insanely small. *Spacious, airy, luxurious* and *grand* all mean insanely small.

- Words matter. It's time to stop prettifying the ugly stuff. *Spousal abuse* means wife beating. *Global warming* means the Earth is toast. *Enhanced interrogation* means torture. And here's a bit of trivia for you: The Bush administration did not coin the phrase *enhanced interrogation*. Nor did it come from Jack Bauer. Nope, it was the Gestapo that originated that little bon mot back in 1937.

- To quote Elmer Fudd, "Be bwave, widdoe wabbit." Take a chance, wear your heart on your sleeve, ask the most attractive man in the room to dance, say what you want, demand what you're entitled to. There's a pretty decent chance that you won't get it, but who will you be if you never even try? Note: Only attempt the dance invitation if there's actual music playing.

- Sometimes I worry that we've all become workaholics—because getting through life can be really hard work. But (with apologies to the fine people who pay my salary every week) we need to log off, go home, and remember what it is to have dinner, conversation, and sex . . . not necessarily in that order.

WAS IT GOOD FOR YOU?

I'M GIVING YOU A choice: We can either (a) discuss the possible privatization of Social Security and its impact on twenty-first century macroeconomics or (b) go shopping for sex toys. May I see a show of hands? Okay, so that would be countless women ready to hit the stores, and one retired stockbroker from the suburbs of Detroit who'd be ever so grateful if I'd start writing for *BusinessWeek*. Sorry, Dad— the people have spoken.

With friends like Hilda Hutcherson, M.D., my go-to sexpert and the author of *Pleasure: A Woman's Guide to Getting the Sex You Want, Need, and Deserve,* who needs sales help? I call my fearless pal and offer to buy her lunch in exchange for a guided tour of the best sex toys currently on the market.

My education begins in the personal massagers section of a discreet midtown Manhattan shop called Eve's Garden. I check out a shelf of architecturally unobtrusive little gadgets as Hilda heads straight for a periwinkle-blue confection. "See how pretty," she says, grouping it with the chartreuse and salmon ones. "They're so sculptural, you could really have them on your coffee table without anyone realizing they're vibrators." But before I can lay out what I feel is a rather cogent argument for not displaying an assortment of pastel sex toys in the middle of my living room, Hilda has moved on. "Ooh, look, Lisa—it's the smoothie!" She picks up an ultrasleek tiger-stripe number and turns it to low. "Smoothies are a bit more phallic," she says as it dawns on me that Hilda's idea of a bit more phallic is my definition of the Washington Monument. "These are terrific for women who are just trying to get their feet wet."

As the smoothie buzzes away, I start to offer her a little free advice: "Technically, Doctor, it's not the feet that need to get—" But before I can finish, Hilda is zeroing in on an odd contraption.

"Here's one based on a medical device for women with arousal disorder. This piece suctions the clitoris," she says, holding up a rubbery thimble, "while this cylinder vibrates. I write lots of prescriptions for these," she says matter-of-factly.

"But isn't everything here over-the-counter?" I ask. "Aren't sex toys more about leisure activity than medical need?" I can't help picturing an operating room in which a dedicated young surgeon calls out for instruments: "Scalpel! Sutures! Box of remote-control panties!"

Hilda puts down the sample of edible Kama Sutra Honey Dust she's been enjoying. "When I write a prescription, I'm giving a woman permission from a doctor," she says. "And some of us need that. Ten percent of the sexually active female population have never had an orgasm, and God knows how many women have trouble climaxing with a partner. I prescribe a vibrator for use during intercourse. Toys give you control and provide extra stimulation."

I wish I'd met Hilda thirty years ago.

Remember kissing with your clothes on? In 1977, a boy named Brad could bring you down to his parents' paneled rec room, put a little Abba on the turntable, toss your algebra homework off the olive green vinyl beanbag chair on which the two of you perched pretending to study, mumble sweet nothings into your newly pierced ear, and from 4:30 to 6:00 P.M., when his stay-at-home mom would call down that dinner was almost ready, that boy could have his way with you. Of course in 1977 "his way" was to dishevel your shag, eat off your Bonne Bell lip gloss, and maybe, *maybe*, if he was a true sexual sophisticate, unhook your Olga bra using nothing more than his left thumb and forefinger.

My partner in crime wasn't actually named Brad and— hell, who are we kidding?— I didn't actually need a bra, but there was a boy and he was on the swim team and he drove a white Trans Am, and in tenth grade that meant something—though, to this day, I'm not exactly sure what. It was Saturday night, the one evening a week when husbands wore leisure suits and wives wore Wind Song, and you'd be left with a pepperoni pizza, a phone number in case of emergency, and a house to yourself, whereupon this sort of gawky, sort of sexy swimmer would appear at the front door, settle into the sofa, and kiss me with his eyes closed for the next three and a half hours. Because back in the day (the day being two years before my current assistant was born), making out wasn't a means to an end, it was an end unto itself. There was no such thing as a good Merlot, a brazen double entendre, a smooth transition to the bedroom. There were only tentative mouths and hungry hands and wild chestnut hair falling all around the Marimekko throw pillows until it was time to stop.

"So, uh, I guess I should get going," said Brad who wasn't Brad.

"Oh, umm, okay," I answered.

I smoothed out my Huckapoo blouse, raised myself up, and reached across him for the Tab on the coffee table. But a funny thing happened on the way to that can of metallic-tasting soda: My arm accidentally grazed his lap. It couldn't have been more innocent, a split second, an inadvertent brush across a pair of button-fly 501s. And yet . . .

"Or," he said (after a slightly startled pause), "I could stay."

Huh? Wait a second, what just happened here? And suddenly I got it! With nothing more than a strong thirst and a light touch, I had gone from coquette to femme fatale. I possessed the power to make him stay!

And there you have it.

Hard to imagine how anyone could have been so naïve, but this was back when I was still a rough draft. It was before we all had to be responsible for our own orgasms, before eHarmony or match.com, Facebook or MySpace, Viagra or Cialis. Rock Hudson was still chunky, Ecstasy was still legal, and foreplay was forever—or at least it was in my little corner of the suburbs.

Hilda just keeps picking sex toys up, then calling out to the cashier for the price. Now, I'm aware that at this point certain readers (and you know who you are, cousin Myrna) would just as soon have me cut to waves pounding against the shore, but for my friends with a healthy curiosity— here goes nothing.

"Hilda," I say, pointing to a gigantic vibrating penis that looks and feels just like the real thing . . . and then some, "you don't think most men would find this a touch daunting?"

"Well, you can always start small. Here," Hilda says, handing me the Fukuoko 9000. "This finger-puppety vibrator slips over any digit, looks totally nonthreatening, and still gets the job done. How could this tiny toy make a man think he's being replaced?" She pauses a beat, shifting into pleasure-activist mode. "But I'm telling you, Lisa, that other one is definitely worth a try. I mean, for one thing, it's dishwasher safe!"

"Thank you, Happy Homemaker."

And on that note, life as I understand it officially ends. I see the sign that informs customers of a 10 percent discount on floor models, I check out the make-your-own-dildo kit containing special molding powder, patented "liquid skin," stir stick, vibrating unit, easy-to-follow instructions, and I suggest we break for lunch.

Over Cobb salads, I ask Hilda if there's any truth to the rumor that vibrators are addictive.

"That's ridiculous," she says. "Granted, if you're using it five or six times a day, it'll be hard to go back—"

"Or hold a job or raise a family or . . . walk," I chime in.

"But," Hilda goes on, "the thing most of us love junkies ache for can't be found in a toy. They've yet to come up with a vibrator that whispers in your ear or holds you tight at three A.M."

"They've yet to come up with a lot of men who do that."

"True, but toys do tend to put the oomph back into long-term relationships, so you start releasing those hormones that actually do keep couples close." Hilda spears a cherry tomato. "And if you don't have a steady partner, they help your body remember how to respond. If you're menopausal—and not sexually active or taking estrogen—they keep the blood flowing through those vessels. You've got to prevent your vagina from shrinking and getting dry—a dildo is fantastic for that," she says as I watch the busboy who's refilling our iced teas go pale and back into a waiter.

"It's a brave new world, my dear," Hilda says as she gives me a hug, gathers her three shopping bags worth of erotica, and heads home to celebrate her husband's fiftieth birthday. With Johannes in Europe, I'm having a girls' night in—just me, Julia, and Angelina Ballerina. Someday Julia will go through my drawers just the way I did my mother's (and by the way, Mom, I now know for a fact that a diaphragm is *not* a kitty cat's bathing cap . . . my first clue being that we didn't have a cat), and who knows what she'll come across. Maybe I'll take that moment to tell her how you have to work at relationships, and how you have to care for yourself, and how—unless you want to be surrounded by a SWAT team and two dozen bomb-sniffing beagles—you have to take the batteries out of toys when you travel. Or maybe I'll just send her out to lunch with Auntie Hilda.

Two days later, I'm Sauvignon Blanc-ing with my friend Laurie when she announces that after almost five respectable weeks of movies, dinners, walks in the park with "adorable, divorced, one-kid-lives-in-Brooklyn, struggling architect guy," the two have finally gone to bed together.

"And did the earth move?" I ask.

"Lisa," my slightly rattled friend replies, "the duvet cover didn't even move."

I do the only thing a person in my position can do: signal the waitress for a dessert menu as my beautiful, size 8 friend admits that he wanted the lights on so he could see her and she wanted the lights off so he couldn't.

Sex—when it's meaningful—can be a sublime expression of love. When it's not, well, it can be even better. And do you know why that is? Neither do I, but that's exactly my point: Sexual pleasure is an elusive little critter. Just when you think you've got it all figured out, something happens— you realize you're in your no-human-being-must-ever-see- these-panties panties, he accidentally elbows you in a way that may require a kidney transplant, the dog appears to be star- ing, the other people on the subway appear to be staring— well, you get the idea.

So once again, I go to my go-to girl for enlightenment. Hilda and I sit down at the little blond wood table in her slightly academic, slightly comfy, very lived-in office and cut straight to the chase.

"I'm mad at women," I tell her.

"Something we said?"

"Sort of. I'm just so sick of nearly everyone I know— myself included—walking around feeling crummy about our bodies to the point that it's actually hard to accept pleasure."

"I know what you mean. If you don't feel at ease with

your body—this package that carries your mind and your soul around every day—then how can you really enjoy anything, especially sex? You're as close as you can be to another human being and instead of feeling his lips, and his fingers, and his heartbeat, you're thinking, *Oh my God, he's near that spot of cellulite by my thigh* or *He's going to realize that my boobs are drooping, that they're not the same size . . ."*

I make a mental note to buy a new bra immediately, and she continues. "It's pretty amazing. I've had patients say, 'I'm only thirty-seven, but I can't have oral sex because I've got gray hair down there and he'll think I'm old.' The things we obsess over."

"So do you prescribe Clairol for those patients?"

"I say, 'Honey, if he's down there doin' that, the last thing on his mind is a little gray hair. He's looking to give you pleasure, and it's up to you to let go and be in the moment.' Another thing I get all the time is, 'I can't have oral sex because I don't think I smell right, or it won't taste good.' I always say, 'Please, tell me how it's supposed to smell. I don't care what the commercials say, it's not supposed to smell like a spring rain or an English garden . . . unless, of course, you're trying to attract bees.' Lisa, do you know what a vagina should smell like?"

"The thing is, Hilda, my parents are still living . . ."

"It should smell like a vagina! It has a natural scent and that scent is there for a reason; it's an aphrodisiac. It's part of the mating ritual. As far as taste goes, how many women have actually taken the time to taste themselves?"

"Umm, I'm gonna say . . . eleven?"

"I encourage women to taste their own secretions, rather

than constantly worrying about them. Self-knowledge makes you more accepting of your body."

"But," I say, both in complete agreement and in desperate need of a subject change, "all the knowledge in the world doesn't guarantee a girl an orgasm."

"You know," she says, filling our coffee cups, "orgasms are intensely pleasurable, but you can't go chasing them. You can't say, 'Okay, if I try really, really hard, I'm going to have an orgasm'—it doesn't work that way."

"How exactly does it work?"

"You have to really concentrate on what all five of your senses are experiencing." Hilda sees my skepticism and elaborates: "When I was in college at Stanford, I liked going to Los Angeles to party. I used to hop in my car and race to get to that party." She smiles. "Then one day, I decided to take the scenic route. It was longer, it was slower, but my God, it was incredible! I remember pulling over, listening to the ocean, looking at the seagulls, smelling the air. I actually forgot all about L.A. I mean, this was the kind of place that makes you believe in a higher power." She seems momentarily lost in the memory. "Anyway, if I had missed the party altogether, the trip would not have been a failure because I took in so much beauty and I had so much fun."

"Let's hear it for the Pacific Coast Highway," I say, getting back to matters at hand.

"All I mean," she continues, "is that pleasure comes in many forms. Your partner may be kissing your earlobes and stroking the back of your knees, but if you're thinking, *He's gotta make me climax or this isn't great sex*, then you're missing out on some extraordinary sensations because your head just isn't in the game. I've got a whole other group of patients who actually do have orgasms but are upset because they're not having *Sex and the City* orgasms."

"Is that where this sort of lightning bolt comes roaring through you at a Manolo Blahnik sale? Because I once saw these scrunchy suede boots in navy, and for a minute there . . ."

Hilda interrupts: "*Sex and the City* was a double-edged sword, and I think we're still feeling its effect. That show obliterated many taboos and got women really talking, but it also made us question ourselves: *How come I've never had that female ejaculation thing that Samantha had?* or *Why aren't I able to achieve multiple orgasms the way those women seem to?*

"I always ask, 'Did the sex leave you feeling good about yourself? Did it leave you feeling connected to your part-ner?' If the answer is yes, then I say quit running after that multiple thing, enjoy the pleasure you *are* having, and go to sleep in his arms."

"Hilda, how did you get so comfortable with all of this?"

"When I started my ob-gyn practice, women would say to me, 'I've heard about this thing called a clitoris, but I don't know where to find it.' Or they'd ask for advice about anal sex, or they'd want to know if there's a vibrator I like. Believe me, I could go on and on."

"I believe you," I say quickly.

"These women forced me to face my own demons. I had to look at all the negative messages that were fed to me over the years. I realized the only way I could help people deal with their issues was if I dealt with my own. So I educated myself into feeling good about my body, good about sex, and free to talk about everything under the sun. I tell my patients, 'If I can go to a sex shop and buy a vibrator, then so can you.'"

"You learned to ask for what you want in bed."

"That's right. And there are all kinds of ways to ask for what you want. Sometimes it's as simple as saying, 'Darling, let's trying something new.' Sometimes it's going out and buying a book of erotica. Sometimes it's putting his hand right where you want it to be and showing him the pressure and tempo that feels good to you." She refills our cups and goes on. "The thing is, if you tell your partner what you want, most of the time you'll get it."

"And if you don't?"

"If someone isn't open to giving you pleasure, then I'd say you're probably with the wrong person." We sit and sip for a minute. Out the window I can see the sky streaked with gray and the students looking a little eager, a little anxious—as though they were born with too much homework. Hilda is the first to speak: "There are an awful lot of reasons in the world to feel bad right now," she says finally. "But how amazing is it that we have this built-in capacity for pure joy?"

And how amazing is it that we also have the Fukuoko 9000?

I AM CURIOUS YELLOW

ON ANY GIVEN DAY at *O* magazine, there are somewhere in the neighborhood of sixty-nine very talented, extremely detail oriented, high-energy, hardworking women and men all doing their jobs and doing them well. I love a few of them, I like a lot of them. I despise one of them. She is the Magneto to my Wolverine, the Saruman to my Frodo, the Dr. Octopus to my Spider-Man. I call her The Tinkler.

It's a typical Tuesday; the office is humming along. I'm answering e-mails, writing cover lines, scheduling a dental appointment here, partial highlights there, kicking myself for not getting sushi at lunch. The sun is shining, the color printer is working—my life is good. I mosey into the ladies' room, glance at the mirror, remind myself that fluorescent lights make everyone look as if they're in the final stages of tuberculosis, and head for a stall. And then I see it: The seat, even the floor, is covered in little yellow droplets. The Tinkler strikes again.

To date, I have been able to deduce only four things about her:

1. She is female.

2. She attacks between the hours of 10 A.M. and 8 P.M.

3. She works alone.

4. She was raised in a barn.

I've been her victim more times than I can count, and it has turned me from a happy-go-lucky columnist into a bitter, paranoid germaphobe. Indeed, she has become the bane of my existence. We live in a world where our soldiers lack sufficient body armor, where Rupert Murdoch is blurring the line intended to keep the business and political interests of media owners from influencing the presentation of news, where the national beverage has become high-fructose corn syrup, where studies indicate that worrying you're going to get sick will get you sick—and yet I am devoting an entire chapter to The Tinkler.

Any shrink worth his or her salt will tell you that it is a mistake to think of your colleagues as family. But what is a family if not a group of people who care about you and irritate you and show up for cake on your birthday and look at pictures of your kid even when they don't feel like it and think it wouldn't kill you to put on a little makeup and a pair of heels once in a while? I've been earning a paycheck for thirty years. Whether rinsing conditioner off a Lhasa apso during my stint as shampoo girl at Mr. Whiskers Pet Boutique or breathing on the chicken breast I was about to serve a rude diner during my waitressing days, I've always found that the people I work with matter to me. Their moods, their opinions, their styles influence my life. I've been appreciated and I've been humiliated, I've been surprised and I've been antagonized. I've gotten flowers and I've gotten fired (and I'm pretty sure I didn't do anything to deserve either), but I've never experienced anything like The Tinkler.

"Dammit!" I say upon encountering her latest Jackson Pollock imitation. Pat, Suzan, and Valerie each comes out of her stall to see what's wrong. I point in horror. Pat groans, Suzan moans, Val throws up her hands in disgust, and we fall into silence. Then I rally, "At least we know it's not one of us." But everybody else is a suspect. "It can't be Sudie," Suzan volunteers. My brow furrows. "What are you basing this on?" I ask. "I've seen her," she answers, "she always heads straight for the paper seat protector." "And," Valerie adds, "we can cross Mamie off the list—it happened twice while she was in Sweden." Sixty seconds ago the four of us were editors; now we are FBI profilers. "She probably likes to burrow into small spaces," Pat conjectures. "This never happens in the big, wheelchair-accessible stall . . ." "It's very primitive, as if she's marking her territory. This is clearly a hostile gesture," Suzan declares with authority. We're finally getting somewhere. "So, really," I say, "we just need to be on the lookout for a mean-spirited, molelike cavewoman who is not confined to a wheelchair . . . is that right?" Val is the first to realize that we're losing our minds. "I'm out of here," she says, and exits the ladies' room.

Later, I complain to J.J., poor naïve little J.J. . . . She tells me that it can't be any of us, that the toilet is somehow to blame. I leave J.J. in her special world—a place where troubles melt like lemon drops and Lee Harvey Oswald acted alone—and resume working. Gina drops by and reads over my shoulder. Suddenly she has an epiphany: "It's you!" she announces, pointing at me like she's Javert accusing Jean Valjean of stealing silver candlesticks. "Think about it," she says. "What better way to cover your tracks than writing an outraged piece on the subject?" I kind of like that Gina believes I am an evil genius, and don't have the heart to tell her that I once refused to sit my daughter on the lap of a department store Santa Claus because I had no idea who else had been sitting there.

Another day, another bathroom break. "Steer clear of the third stall," Yeun warns as she dries her hands and heads out for a meeting. Jennifer emerges from door number four to see what exactly is going on behind door number three. She is appalled yet philosophical. "Believe it or not, every place I've ever worked has had a Tinkler—maybe sharing a ladies' room just sends certain people into a passive-aggressive snit. It's the dark side of office life."

Lately, my daydreams bear a striking resemblance to one of those black-and-white Sherlock Holmes movies: The entire staff sits, sipping brandy in an ornate drawing room. "I suppose you're wondering why I've gathered you here today," I begin in an inexplicable British accent. "Well, my friends, one of you is The Tinkler." The research department averts its eyes. The art department fidgets nervously. An intern gasps. "And," I go on, "nobody is leaving this room until I reveal the person who refuses to work and play well with others." My assistant, Polly, looks up. "You mean you've figured out the identity of The Tinkler?" she asks, filled with an admiration for my powers of reasoning that she has never once expressed in real life. "It was elementary, dear Watson. I merely——" but before I can unmask The Tinkler or explain why I refer to Polly as Dear Watson, the lights suddenly go out and an ear-splitting scream fills the parlor.

I could go on, but I'm bored silly whenever someone feels compelled to relay every nanosecond of a dream. Suffice it to say that I usually wind up in the arms of Tyrone Power. As for The Tinkler? She's still on the lam.

There are lots of days when I find myself wishing life were closer to one of those movies from the 1930s——women wore fabulous hats and pearl chokers, and I don't think they actually went to the bathroom back then. They were too busy dancing with Fred Astaire and smoking unfiltered cigarettes to schlep to an office every day. Now some of us are running the offices, but it seems we've brought a few low-grade lunatics along for the ride——and they're wreaking havoc in the ladies' room. Where have you gone, Edith Wharton—— our nation turns its bloodshot eyes to you. I'm not asking for cloth napkins and classical music. I don't need a mint on my pillow. I just want to go to work each day and find a bit of common courtesy, a modicum of civility, a touch of class, or failing all that, a magnum of Lysol.

25

𝒫AGING AMY VANDERBILT

So I'm on an elevator, minding my own business, when I hear a series of quick metallic clicks coming from behind me. Incongruous . . . yet somehow familiar. It's the sound of fingernails being clipped! I can think of only two circumstances in which clipping one's fingernails on an elevator might be socially acceptable: if said elevator is located in the privacy of your own bathroom, or if there actually happens to be a tiny nail salon in the rear of the elevator. "Perhaps I lack a certain devil-may-care, live-and-let-live mentality, but I don't feel like spending the rest of the morning wondering if a stranger's discarded pinky nail is clinging to the back of my sweater," I complain to Mamie, my like-minded colleague. "I know," she says. "I once witnessed a woman attempting to pluck her eyebrows while hailing a cab on Broadway."

What's with all this public preening? How did it get to be illegal to drive using a cell phone, yet perfectly okay to apply mascara at sixty miles an hour? Since when has riding the subway become our special time to check for blackheads—and, yes, on a particularly memorable trip to Union

Square, an opportunity for one highly motivated passenger to wax her legs? Am I exaggerating? Only a select group on Manhattan's downtown N train knows for sure. I think my friend Dave put it best when, upon witnessing a woman at the farmers' market with an upper lip covered in Jolene cream, he posed this simple question: Are women nuts? I wanted to defend us, but there she was, plain as day, publicly bleaching her mustache while tapping a Crenshaw melon for signs of ripeness. Have we no shame? Shouldn't there be a few guidelines where this stuff is concerned? Allow me:

1. There are two schools of thought on the lipstick-at-the-dinner-table question. According to *The Amy Vanderbilt Complete Book of Etiquette*, "Many women instinctively reach for their lipstick at the end of a meal. Whatever you do, resist the urge." Frankly, I can go either way on the lipstick issue. Retiring to the ladies' room is certainly more gracious, but I'm not especially offended when someone discreetly (no liner, no blending six shades, no topcoat of gloss) touches up her lipstick as the table is being cleared. Incidentally, you may also feel free to steam open your pores using an entrée of salmon en papillote, but remember that it is never okay to follow up with toner, moisturizer, under-eye cream, Retin-A, and Restylane injections.

2. Let's say we're at the gym and you need to borrow shampoo. Fine by me. I'll even throw in my Frédéric Fekkai conditioner for color-treated, dry, or damaged hair. Really, go ahead and ask—but do your asking

with a towel on! Here's the deal: We change our clothes quickly in the locker room, we frolic naked leisurely in *Sorority Sex Kittens Part Two*.

3. Which brings me to another point: You know how people are constantly saying, "Don't be shy"? People are wrong. Be shy, be *very* shy. There's a reason I did not go to medical school . . . okay, there are two reasons: (1) My shockingly low grades; and (2) I have absolutely no desire to do a quick mole check for you, hear the details of your yeast infection, or dig through your scalp for head lice. That's why God invented doormen.

4. I've attended dinners at which, so help me God, otherwise civilized women take the arrival of dessert and coffee as an opportunity to run a quick brush through their hair. Repeat after me: Pumpkin mousse and Suave Volumizing mousse do not mix.

5. When out and about, please refrain from combing, brushing, blushing, pinching, poking, weaving, lining, coating, frosting, pushing, pulling, plumping, nipping and tucking. Bottom line: You look fabulous—and if you don't, well, darling, it's too late now. Let's leave ourselves alone.

26

ℐILL SLEEP DO US PART

I HAD THE FLU. But not just any flu. No, this was the kind of bug that forces a normally rational human being to dial information and beg the operator for Jack Kevorkian's home phone number. This was the kind that leaves a generally-well-groomed woman crumpled on the sofa in her rattiest flannel nightgown, the one that her seventy-nine-year-old aunt from Detroit presented with the keen observation: "Magenta puppies always make things look zanier." Such was my state when Johannes walked in. "Man," he called out while hanging his coat in the front hall closet. "I've never seen so many beautiful women in one city . . ." The love of my life continued from the foyer, "I mean, it's like a convention of supermodels out there—" He rounded the corner just in time to watch me sneeze cherry Jell-O over the Arts & Leisure section. "But," he stammered, "none as beautiful as you, my angel."

"Avert your eyes, for I am hideous," I whimpered à la the Elephant Man.

"No, seriously, you look . . . not horrible," which was

SOMEONE WILL BE WITH YOU SHORTLY

true, provided you're drawn to individuals who appear to have combed peanut butter through their hair. Finally, in what can only be described as a genuinely pathetic effort to change the subject, he added, "So, I'm just curious. When was the last time you, uh, you know . . . showered?" I gathered up my Sudafed, my Mucinex, my Puffs, my honey-and-lemon cough drops, my lip balm, my thermometer, my blanket, my *TV Guide*, my diet ginger ale, my wonton soup, my cordless phone, my few remaining shards of dignity, and with all the icy élan a woman dressed in a soup-stained frolicking-puppy print can muster, I replied, "Good day, sir!" He tried for a last-minute save: "Are you losing weight?" But I cut him off. "I said good day!" and flounced (okay, I tripped over the vaporizer) to our bedroom, where I proceeded to lapse in and out of seven back-to-back episodes of *Dexter*.

When I was extremely young and shockingly stupid, I thought you weren't supposed to ever get angry at anybody you cared about (lest you suspect I'm exaggerating the "shockingly stupid" part, I also thought Mount Rushmore was a natural phenomenon). I honestly believed that people who were truly in love would never dream of having a good, old-fashioned, knock-down, drag-out fight. I guess when you're the type of girl who walks around thinking that the wind just sort of sculpted Teddy Roosevelt into the side of a mountain, the concept of a fairy-tale relationship makes total sense. Johannes and I don't have a fairy-tale relationship. Try as we might, we just can't persuade my co-op board to let us install a moat. So no, the life we've designed isn't perfect, but I've never been a big fan of perfection—it's a bitch to achieve and impossible to maintain. Instead, we argue on a semiregular basis. Sometimes we look back at the tougher moments and laugh—the influenza incident of 2001, the would-it-kill-you-to-go-that extra-step-from-the-sink-to-the-dishwasher episode of last Tuesday—and sometimes we get mad all over again. But when Johannes fights, he fights like a grown-up. He isn't mean, he isn't sarcastic, he isn't out to annihilate. He just wants us to order in Thai food, watch MSNBC, and be friends again.

Loving somebody and then having the guts to let them love you back is a lot harder than it sounds. At least it is for me. For the first three years of our life together I kept waiting for him to rip off his Mr. Nice Guy mask and turn into everybody who ever broke my heart. I poked, I prodded, I harangued, I guilted, I entrapped, I tested, I stopped just short of waterboarding. But Johannes refused to take the bait. Instead, he maintained his calm, retained his benevolence, and developed migraines.

He made sure I understood that he was in it for the long haul; I would never again have to sit on a blind date listening to some guy tell me what Pink Floyd was really trying to say on *Dark Side of the Moon*. The man makes me feel loved—even when he hates me. And that, I've come to realize, is no small thing.

I have a friend, we'll call her Jane because Jane is a charming, classic name. Jane is married to this guy, let's call him Dick because, well, suffice it to say the name suits him perfectly. I've had fun with Dick and Jane; we've gone to the theater and dinner and a couple of Knicks games together. Because Johannes is so frequently in Europe, I became like a little dinghy tied to the boat of their marriage, just kind of bobbing along behind them in case of an emergency. One Sunday a few years ago, we were brunching in TriBeCa— because before there were kids and cartoons and Honey Nut Cheerios, there was sleep and sex and brunches in TriBeCa. Anyway, Jane knocked over her water glass, prompting Dick to spend the rest of the meal excoriating her for every single misstep she'd ever made. He opened his rant with "Christ, it's excruciating to sit next to you at a table," and closed with a reference to her "fat idiot mother." Check please!

Jane called the next morning to apologize for making me part of their *Who's Afraid of Virginia Woolf?* production. I wanted to say, You're not the one who should be sorry. I wanted to say, Your only mistake was in not lobbing the basket of stale sweet rolls at his head—the cheese danish alone was heavy enough to stun him into silence. I wanted to say, Janey, Janey, Janey, what's become of your self-respect? I wanted to say, It's not whether somebody loves you (I mean, for all I know O.J. loved Nicole), it's how he treats you that counts. I found myself wondering: Is Jane afraid to be alone? Is it a money thing? Maybe she's an unindicted co-conspirator, provoking him in some way that I'm just not seeing? Or maybe she woke up one morning and twenty-three years and two sons had simply come and gone—right along with her energy and confidence. Maybe she just forgot who she'd wanted to be when she grew up. In the end all I managed was, "I'm here if you need me."

"What's the matter? Are you coming down with some-thing?" Johannes asks as I crawl into bed. I assure him that I'm fine. "Then why are you wearing the magenta puppy nightgown of death?" I explain that I'm working on a column and it's got me thinking about him and me and Dick and Jane and love and homicide and that point when a working relationship becomes more work than relationship. I admit there are moments when I'm not sure if it's luck or love or fear of failure that keeps us going, and I ask Johannes if he knows what I mean. There is a very long pause. He is contemplative. He is introspective. He is sound asleep.

27

𝒯RUTH OR DARE

THE STORY GOES THAT as a child George Washington chopped down the backyard cherry tree and then admitted the whole sordid affair to his beloved father: "I cannot tell a lie," he is said to have said. "It was I who chopped down your cherry tree." This leads me to a couple of thoughts: First, had Xbox been around in the 1700s, I like to think George would've been too zombied out on Guitar Hero to have ever left the sofa, let alone go all lumberjacky on an innocent bit of landscaping. Second, what were the Washingtons thinking? Color me cautious, but I've never been a big believer in allowing children direct access to an ax. Ditto hatchets, swords, tomahawks, muskets, and Barbie. Second, I cannot tell a lie; had I been in that very same situation, there's no doubt in my mind that I'd have looked my beloved father straight in the eye and told a lie. And that, along with the wooden teeth and powdered wig, is what separates me from our first president. I could tell you I believe it is imperative that we be absolutely meticulous with the truth 100 percent of the time, but the truth is—I'd be lying.

You see, I live in New York City, where manhole covers explode and construction cranes crash from the sky and people slip through the space between the subway platform and the train, and you feel almost giddy with relief on those days when you manage to make it home in one piece. The bottom line is this: Life is short, time is precious, and I don't want to spend Saturday night watching my friend, the would-be actress, do a walk-on in *Tartuffe*. It's not that I don't love my friend, and it's not that I don't love *Tartuffe* (okay, that's a lie, nobody loves *Tartuffe*). It's just that I reserve Saturday night for slathering my reptilelike feet in Vaseline Intensive Care as my daughter shampoos her American Girl doll in the kitchen sink. But try explaining that to a friend who has just spent $200 on a brocade bustle and is flying her parents in from Wisconsin for her off-off-off Broadway debut. My choices? Well, I can sit through *Tartuffe* with a lovely couple from Racine and a running time of two hours and forty-six minutes that I'll never get back. I can pray that one of my undermoisturized feet will suddenly fossilize so that I can use it to knock myself unconscious. Or I can say, "Darn the luck, that's the night I have to . . ." Fill in fiendishly fabricated excuse here. And, yes, I know, this makes me sound kind of awful, but I ask that you refrain from judging me until you've endured an evening of musical theater based on the early years of Joseph Goebbels, courtesy of this same friend.

Honesty is a delightful policy, but if we're going to be honest, you have to admit that without at least a few lies, Thanks-

SOMEONE WILL BE WITH YOU SHORTLY

giving with the family would be a thing of the past, first dates would end before your second white wine spritzer makes it to the table, every political figure who intentionally linked Iraq with Osama bin Laden would be forced to resign in disgrace (yes, even retroactively), and plastic surgeons throughout the greater Los Angeles area would end their lives in the gutter holding large cardboard signs that read WILL BOTOX FOR FOOD.

Ask any man in a healthy relationship, and he will tell you that when his wife comes home with a horrific haircut, it's a mistake to start feverishly skimming the Yellow Pages for an attorney while muttering, "I think we've got a lawsuit here. The bastard who did this to you will never trim bangs in this town again!" No, he must greet her with the simple phrase that I've already told you my sweetheart uses to chill me out whenever I despair. Johannes will look up from whatever he's doing, pause, tilt his head, then casually ask: "Are you losing weight?"

COUPLEHOOD: A BRIEF ONE ACT

Lisa: *Plastic is destroying the earth!*

Johannes: Are you losing weight?

L: *The creepy guy who hangs out on Second Avenue followed me into Dunkin' Donuts to announce that I remind him of a young Kim Jong-il!*

J: Are you losing weight?

L: *I've put on three pounds since breakfast!*

J: Are you losing weight?

What can I say? He's lying. I know he's lying and yet it works for us. I am also a firm believer in lying to chatty cabdrivers ("Yep, back when I was a CIA operative, the only thing a girl needed to take care of business was a poisoned umbrella tip and a can-do attitude"), my dental hygienist ("Let's see, I suppose I'm brushing five, maybe six, times a day actually"), and my kid ("Bambi's mother is alive and well. She has merely relocated to a breathtaking piece of beachfront property off the coast of Hawaii with her hunky new boyfriend, Raul, who is both incredibly wealthy and keenly aware of her every need"). To this day, Julia believes that Toys "R" Us is only open when my parents visit Manhattan; the shelves are stocked as Grandma and Grandpa's plane touches down and the doors to the store lock as soon as they head back to the airport.

Here is the truth, the whole truth, and nothing but the truth: My name is Lisa and I am a liar, though a good marketing consultant could probably finesse the word into something a bit more palatable: "Reality Stylist" might be good, or "Pinocchiotologist" could work. My mother insists that, at the end of the day, what I am is a storyteller—and she might have a point. Joan Didion says that "we tell ourselves stories in order to live." I think that's right. Forget what I tell cabdrivers for sport or dental hygienists for spin control or *Bambi* readers for peace of mind. It's the lies we tell ourselves that determine the particular arc of our stories. I tell myself that it's never too late to master Italian and piecrust, that one day I'll appreciate Clay Aiken and understand calculus. I tell myself that I'll be able to guarantee my daughter a life of joy and confidence and financial security in

SOMEONE WILL BE WITH YOU SHORTLY

a universe that's just and safe and green. To be honest, I have my doubts. Perhaps I was born predisposed to pessimism or maybe I've witnessed too much pain, but my mind is forever taking me to the dark side and I am afraid of the dark. So I sugarcoat and I gloss over, and I rationalize and, yes, I sometimes fictionalize my little story. I tell rose-colored lies because Lexapro doesn't always get the job done, because I want with all my heart to believe in something just a bit cheerier than what I see on the six o'clock news. And because, to tell you the truth, I've always been a sucker for a happy ending—even if it means my pants catch fire.

28

"WHAT THE HELL KIND OF BRA ARE YOU WEARING?"

IT STARTED WITH AN untucked shirt. I mean, you put on a pound or two and you want to be comfortable, right? And maybe hide out in something just a little on the baggy side—that seems perfectly reasonable, doesn't it? And clogs are so easy to slip into—nobody really notices shoes, do they? Besides, Julia needs breakfast and the sitter is running late, and I've got to get to the office and who has time to deal with accessories or makeup . . . or one's reflection in a full-length mirror? Yep, it started with an untucked shirt, and before anybody could say, "Stevie Nicks: the chunky years," the baby was ready for kindergarten and I had taken up residence in Schlumpadinka City.

I tell myself that it's obscene and vain and idiotic to think about personal style when the world is falling apart. This despite my mother's pointed observation that "refusing to put on a pair of tailored trousers probably isn't doing all that much for the Iraqi people." Here is the truth: I allowed myself to gain weight, and maybe as a punishment, or maybe as a form of denial, or maybe because I just couldn't find plus-sized clothes that corresponded to the way I wanted to look (simple, sleek, modern, with just a hint of bling), I gave up on trying to look any way at all. I stopped paying attention to myself and hoped everyone else would have the decency to do the same.

Enter Adam Glassman. One part angel of mercy, one part dictatorial devil, all parts swathed in cashmere. Adam is the creative director of *O* magazine. But his influence doesn't stop there. The man is on a personal crusade to keep America beautiful. He will point out when your hair is too big. He will come to your home and angle your sofa. He will let you know if your hemline dips too low or your heels reach too high. To paraphrase *Monsters Inc.*, he scares because he cares.

We are sitting in his office, reviewing a layout. "Adam," I begin, "what makes this particular sandal so special?" He answers my question with another question: "What the hell kind of bra are you wearing?"

The rest is sort of a blur. All I can tell you is phone calls were placed, clothes were brought in, measurements were taken, and I suddenly find myself in a busy Madison Avenue shop aptly named Intimacy, where Dee (a.k.a. the Miracle Worker) ushers me into a dressing room, looks me up and down, declares me a 36E (who knew?), and proceeds to fit me in every bra style ever devised. Now it's time for the body shapers. Suddenly Dee is Hattie McDaniel and I am Scarlett O'Hara getting my corset strings pulled till breathing no longer feels like a viable option. "My husband always helps me get into this one," she says with a Herculean tug. "Does your husband live near me?" I ask feebly. We settle on a lightweight little Spanx number called Higher Power. God may be good, but *this* higher power flattens my tummy.

The next day I walk into the office (though technically my chest arrives about seven seconds before the rest of me makes it off the elevator) and receive the following news from Polly, my unflappable assistant. "Adam stopped by." I hang up my jacket, grab a bottle of water, and reach for my glasses. "He probably wants to go over the schedule," I murmur as I click on the morning's first e-mail. Polly shakes her head. "He said he just wanted to look at your boobs."

All righty, then.

I walk the girls over to his place and am greeted with instant approval. "Whoa!" he says. "You're narrower and straighter!" I have impressed Adam Glassman, and life is sweet! "Your blouse isn't gaping at the bust anymore, and you've obviously gotten into your Higher Power. You now have a proper foundation. Do you know what this means, Lisa?" I know serving red wine with fish is generally frowned upon. I know Denny McLain pitched for the Detroit Tigers in 1968. I know love means never having to say you're sorry. "What does it mean, Adam?" "It means we can get down to business."

Business begins with Adam asking me to describe my look honestly. I think for a long, long time. "Well, I guess I'm doing a second-trimester bohemian Greek widow kind of thing." He smiles—we've been friends for a lot of years. "I mean, I know the flowing earth-mother stuff just makes me look bigger . . . it might even make me look like I'm off to slaughter a goat in some weird religious rite—but I don't know how to fix it." I can feel my eyes welling up and my neck getting blotchy, but I forge ahead. "For starters, it's hard to look polished in these pathetic grandma shoes—where do I find anything even remotely sexy in extra wide? How do I find bracelets that fit my wrists? And clothes are so expensive," I say as my whine climbs the shrillness scale. "I've seen jeans that cost a couple of hundred dollars, not that they'd even fit me, and . . ." Adam nods in that way people nod when it dawns on them that they're trapped in a confined space with a crumbling crazy lady. "Take a breath, honey." He is calm but definitive as he slips me a Kleenex. "I'm way ahead of you."

He leads me to the fashion closet (which happens to be larger than my living room), where a rack of clothes is ready and waiting. He puts me in a little black dress—but it's sleeveless and I am horrified. "I won't show my upper arms and you can't make me!" I wail. He quells my hysteria with a purple cardigan and prescribes nightly bicep curls. Then he hands me a crystal necklace, black stockings, and a pair of heels he found on the Internet in an extra wide—and it all comes together. "The dress is double knit," he points out, "which holds you in a bit more." I'm wondering which organ I can put up on eBay to buy that dress. "And," he adds, "it's from Old Navy." He throws a tweed car coat with a funnel-neck collar over the dress: "This works with everything." He hands me another Old Navy dress—a jersey wrap. I don't love it, and I say so, but Adam instructs me to hang on, does some pinning to tighten the sleeves, and puts me back in my heels. "Okay, look again," he commands. I'm shocked by the difference. "You see, Lisa, sometimes a little tailoring takes a piece from just okay to fantastic. Notice how the skirt has some fluidity, how gracefully it moves with you; look at the way your underwear is smoothing everything out." I nod in amazement. "Great! Now quit rushing to judgment before we've even got your shoes and jewelry on." I try gray slacks with an elongating pinstripe and top it with a silky print tunic. "The bejeweled V-neck creates the illusion of a leaner torso and draws attention up to your face. This is perfect for the holidays," he assures me.

He puts me in a sharp black suit from Calvin Klein that drapes beautifully, and he insists I can wear the jacket with jeans. "Adam, I can't wear jeans—if they fit in the waist, they're baggy in the thighs and ass." He explains that this is because I'm not a plus size everywhere, that my thighs and bottom are actually pretty slender. It is a quote I plan to have engraved on my tombstone: "Here lies Lisa Kogan and her bony ass." It gives me the strength to try seven-teen different jeans until a high-rise skinny-legged pair by a brand called Evans does the trick. Eureka! He pairs them with my new favorite top, a soft cotton jersey tunic with a bead-embellished scoop neckline (built-in jewelry!) and the Calvin jacket. We are both a little giddy with success. If I didn't know better, I'd say I was thin. I do, however, know better—the fact is, I'm not thin. But here's my newfound reality: You don't have to be thin to look good.

Actually, this was not my first rodeo. Truth be told, I've had one other makeover, and yes, I'm smiling as I remember it.

Right around my thirty-sixth birthday, I stood staring dumbfounded into the mirror as my fingertip skimmed over a fine line around my mouth that seemed to have come out of nowhere. This was my face; I knew its geography better than any other. It had betrayed me on more than one occasion—slow to look contrite during a scolding, quick to heat up when a little bit of cool would be a godsend. I'd gotten my father's forehead and my mother's chin. The adjective *willowy* had never been used to describe my body and there were days when Moses couldn't part my hair, but generally speaking I was pretty okay with how I looked.

Except for one thing . . . one major, horrible, nasty thing: I had lousy teeth.

As a toddler in the early sixties, I was treated with the antibiotic tetracycline. Unfortunately, there was a side effect: It left my teeth mottled and dark—tiger's-eye, really—and me unable to smile without being completely self-conscious. What do the photos of trout fishing up north, the night we got our dog, and my seventh birthday party have in common? In every shot, my lips are locked together as I resolutely refuse to say cheese.

Twice a year, I'd beg the dentist to do something and twice a year he'd assure me that dentistry was evolving and a solution would soon present itself. Then came bonding. I was in junior high, *really* not smiling, when my dentist decided to make me his guinea pig. Lord knows he tried his best, and certainly it was an improvement, but the bonding regularly chipped and the color had an icky grayish cast. Still, as the years went by I learned to live with it, partly because elective cosmetic dentistry is not covered by insurance, partly because I was waiting for that big revolution to kick in, and—let's be honest here—partly because where dental work is concerned, I'm a big scaredy-cat.

Enter Larry Rosenthal, D.D.S., or rather Rosenthal's publicist, with his offer to perform a state-of-the-art procedure in exchange for a magazine article describing it. I'd always heard that if you're in the market for porcelain veneers (facings, thin as a baby's fingernail, that are bonded with a laser or plasma arc light to the surface of teeth), Rosenthal was the man to see.

I arrived for my consultation expecting your basic waiting room: last month's magazines, not enough coat hangers, a receptionist who wished she'd stayed in school. Instead I found an office full of patients and staff schmoozing contentedly over stacks of before-and-after photos. I kept thinking there was something slightly odd about all those people . . . and then it hit me. These were Stepford patients. They were evangelical in their enthusiasm—born again smile fanatics worshipping at the altar of the Rosenthal Group.

Before I could make a run for it, I was ushered into Rosenthal's inner sanctum and in whirled the good doctor himself. He showed me half a dozen love-struck letters from satisfied patients as others popped their heads in to say a quick hello or air-kiss him goodbye. Each one grinned broadly and told me how delighted I was going to be. He introduced me to his two partners, Peter Rinaldi and Robert DiPilla, and explained that they worked as a team. He hopped out of his chair to greet another satisfied customer, demonstrate the latest high-tech dental gizmo, practice his golf swing. He grabbed a call from Greece, another from Paris. Fifteen minutes went by, during which I thought he barely noticed me. I was wrong.

"So, Lisa," he said, his voice suddenly soft. "Do you know how many times you've managed to put your hand in front of your mouth as you've been sitting here?"

The gesture had become second nature to me—and of course he'd caught it.

"You have really good skin and big green eyes, but I think we can make your teeth your strongest feature."

He explained that veneers allowed for more precision in contouring the teeth than bonding. Because my face was (and still is) round, he wanted to lengthen my boxy teeth, which would create a more slenderizing effect overall. We decided to do eight of my top teeth. He proposed building them out a bit, to make my upper lip fuller and more distinctly bowed. So far, so good.

"I want them blindingly white," I announced.

"No," Rosenthal said, probably for the millionth time, "you want them blindingly beautiful, and that means the color has to relate to your hair, your eyes, your skin tone. You don't want to look like you've got a mouth full of Chiclets. You don't want people wondering what you did to yourself. You just want a beautiful smile."

One week later, I showed up for the first step of my three-part procedure in loose, comfortable clothing, having eaten a hearty breakfast, just as the pre-op instructions advised. It was going to be a long day. (Somehow the word *pre-op* had failed to register on my nervous system. If I thought for a minute that I was having an actual surgical procedure, I'd have been a wreck, but I'd watched *ER* for years and I'd yet to see Noah Wylie floss anyone.) Besides, I'd asked if the procedure would involve shots and was told that it would not, so I was perfectly calm.

The procedure involved shots. A lot of them. Rinaldi said something about wanting to reshape my gum line with a laser. I said something about wanting my mommy, and next thing I knew, I was numb. An impression of my mouth was taken. A photo of my mouth holding a rubber dam was taken. My last shred of dignity was taken. DePilla came by to lend a hand as Rinaldi removed my old bonding. Rosenthal dropped in to complain about the choice of background music. He showed me a picture of his incredibly cute son. He told me how his grandmother once asked him if he been "smoking the marinara." I laughed despite myself. There was a method to their madness: I was so busy listening to the Three Amigos that slowly my hands stopped gripping the armrests.

Now it was time for Rosenthal to experiment with various shapes and colors of temporary veneers by placing them over my teeth. The clowning around ceased. He was utterly focused. All three dentists whispered back and forth, holding samples of porcelain up to my teeth. "Too stark," said one. "That's reading a little pink," said another. "Less opaque," said the third. Ultimately, the ceramicist would study photos of my face, consult with Rosenthal, and blend colors to develop the right white. For now, these temporaries were a vast improvement over the teeth I walked in with. I was told to return Monday afternoon for the permanents and to make it a weekend of soft food.

Five hours and one relatively spongy muffin later, my two front veneers had cracked in half diagonally and I'd become Hillbilly Helen, the Clampett nobody talks about. I was horrified by my own vanity, but I spent the weekend as a shut-in. "When you speak of this—and you will—try to be kind," was the only thing I said as I paid my one and only visitor: the man who delivers soup and pad thai.

By Monday morning, I had picked away at the other veneers, creating a jack-o'-lantern effect seldom seen outside of the film *oeuvre* of Wes Craven. The team was not alarmed. They only smiled and told me that it would save a little time. I did not smile back. They scraped off the remaining resin and began the complex process of cementing, shaping, trimming, and polishing my custom-made veneers.

"What if these come off, too?" I asked.

"That's highly unlikely," replied the hygienist. "These should last a good fifteen years unless maybe somebody kicks you in the face."

I made a mental note never to antagonize Jackie Chan.

The goal was perfection, and perfection meant building in a few tiny flaws to keep the porcelain from looking artificial. Each tooth got a bit of shading to provide a dimensional quality. Subtle striations were incorporated, square edges were curved, the veneers were laser-bonded into place. No needles were necessary. At last someone handed me a mirror. Slowly I brought it to my face. I smiled tentatively. I put down the mirror, then picked it up again and shot a fast grin. I leaned the mirror upright against a counter, walked away, pretended a friend was calling to me, pivoted, and flashed an enormous grin as I greeted the mirror. The transformation was shocking. I floated out of the office and smiled my way up Park Avenue.

Over the next two weeks, my doorman asked if I got a haircut. My dry cleaner said I'd lost weight. I posed for my passport photo sans Ativan.

At our final appointment, Rosenthal did a little fine-tuning, told me about the future of dental care, suggested I consider switching to red lipstick, and introduced me to a slightly apprehensive-looking first timer.

I immediately began to gush, explaining how a lifelong inhibition had been eradicated in a matter of days, then deftly demonstrated the dramatic contrast with my yucky teeth in back and the new porcelain-coated ones in front. I went on at some length about how painless the process was, how much I idolized all three doctors, how amazed I was each time I passed a mirror.

She asked me if I was familiar with the Stockholm syndrome.

"You mean that thing where the hostage starts worshipping her captor? See how *you* feel after three sessions," I said with a high-voltage smile. What else could I say, I'd become one of those zealots I tended to sidestep at cocktail parties—a true believer—a smile fanatic.

29

ℛEASONS TO LIVE

IT'S PROBABLY GOOD THAT I'm not rich. Money, it seems to me, sends people in one of three directions: It accelerates an innate inclination to be generous, or it accelerates a kamikaze inclination to party with the Olsen twins, or it sucks away your sense of purpose, and produces a desperate need to eat nothing but those little white Cheddar Cheez-It crackers while staring blankly at an endless cycle of *Everybody Loves Raymond* reruns. I like to think that if I were rich, I'd be the kind of person who looks at the world and decides to fund cancer research and build schools and feed the hungry, and save whoever needs saving, but there's an excellent chance I'd be the kind of person who looks at the world and decides never to get out of bed again. In fact, despite my very real (and utterly inconvenient) need to earn a living, I'm still the kind of person who leans toward the whole Cheez-It thing.

To begin with, I have a slight tendency toward depression (think Morticia Addams downloading an acoustic set from Leonard Cohen). And when this particular brain chemistry is confronted with the incredibly unsettling knowledge that people no longer work like dogs to get ahead, they work like dogs just to stay where they are, well, a girl starts needing a few good reasons to get up, put on a little lipstick, and venture out. But it's no secret that it's not pretty out there. Food prices are soaring, the housing market is plummeting, the middle class is disappearing, the mosquitoes are winning, and Madonna is touring. This is all the more reason to keep a soothing thought or two close at hand. Someday soon, I promise, we can sit down together and come up with a breathtaking bucket list that finally commits us to skydiving with Morgan Freeman just as we've secretly prayed we would, but today I'm offering a different kind of list.

GOOD REASONS TO PUT ON A LITTLE LIPSTICK AND VENTURE OUT (OR AT LEAST PUT ON CLEAN PAJAMAS AND RAISE YOUR WINDOW SHADE A COUPLE OF INCHES):

- Junior high is just one long daisy chain of nonstop mean, and you have officially survived it. That's right, you may have to face locusts, drought, World War III, and the Great Depression II, but you can now go forth secure in the understanding that seventh grade is over. You get to wake up each and every morning without worrying that Arleen Posner got the same Frye boots as you. You will never have to read *Jude the Obscure*, be groped by a thirteen-year-old reeking of his father's Aqua Velva, or feather your bangs again. The enormity of this revelation must not be underestimated.

- Javier Bardem walks among us.

- My delightfully decadent friend Stephen Whitlock recently discovered a recipe for bacon ice cream (www .davidlebovitz.com), and get this—the first step involves candying the bacon! Let's all take a moment of hushed reverence to contemplate this. First came the polio vaccine, then Neil Armstrong made a giant leap for mankind, and today we actually have the technology to combine pork fat with butter fat, salty with sweet, crunchy with creamy. I firmly believe that what chicken soup does for the common cold, bacon ice cream will one day do for the premenstrual woman.

- One word: Spanx. We can now have our scoop of bacon ice cream and wear a clingy Diane von Fursten-berg jersey wrap dress, too.

- Intelligent, witty, creative women appear to be on the rise. I like men. I like men so much that I even had a baby with one of 'em, but the baby is now in first grade, and it's nice to be able to show her some brilliantly talented females—Rachel Maddow (my favorite MSNBC host), Mindy Kaling (playwright, producer, actress, *The Office*), Janice Lee (her debut novel, *The Piano Teacher,* was an absolute knockout)— who are very good at what they do. As role models go, Dora the Explorer only takes a mom so far . . . besides, check out Dora's expressionless little brow— I'm pretty sure it's coursing with Botox.

- Tony Soprano is either dead or eating onion rings, but

Don Draper is alive and mesmerizing every week on *Mad Men*.

- You know those little stain-remover pens that everybody keeps in their bags and desk drawers? I couldn't care less about them. Life is inherently messy and I accept the odd spot of grape juice as part of God's great plan for me and the vast majority of my T-shirts. But the other night at our local diner when Julia accidentally catapulted her chocolate milk shake across our booth, there was my pal Valerie, dry cleaner's pen, ice water, and paper napkins at the ready. Val is just one of those intuitive, insightful, ironic, wildly generous, deeply wonderful people who, despite working two jobs, is quietly, unequivocally there for the people she loves. If you need a complex carbohydrate, she's got the whole grain pasta salad. If you need a sock puppet for your kid's class project, she's got the glue gun. If you need a boost, she's got the ceramic vase brimming with sunflowers. The woman once went on vacation, and I was absolutely bereft. Two weeks without Valerie Soll feels like a house without books.

You see, Javier Bardem, bacon ice cream, and all the mad men in the world don't change the hard truth that plans frequently fail and dreams have been known to dim. But come the morning, there are your friends offering sweet salvation and good gossip and the occasional glass of Sauvignon Blanc with lunch. If ever there was a reason for hope, I guess maybe that's it.

IT'S MY PARTY—AND I'LL MAKE WITTY, ALBEIT POSSIBLY INAPPROPRIATE AND/OR OFFENSIVE REMARKS—IF I WANT TO

"I'M THINKING OF THROWING a little party," I tell my pal Karen as I hold the phone with one hand and fold a mountain of laundry with the other. "No big thing, really, just a few old friends getting together for the holidays," I persist over the dead silence on the other end of the receiver. "Maybe you and Daniel, me and Johannes, and four or five other people who—"

"Daniel and I can't make it," she answers before I can finish.

"But I haven't given you the date."

"Look, Lisa, you know I've had health issues," she counters nervously. I explain to Karen that the American Medical Association has yet to classify "exceedingly dry cuticles" as the kind of condition that requires actual bed rest. "Still . . ." she mutters as her voice trails off.

That night in bed, I turn to Johannes (official party co-host). "Honey, I was thinking it's time we throw a little party," I venture.

"That sounds great, sweetheart."

"Really, pumpkin?"

"Of course, angel. I do have one small request, though."

"Anything, lamb chop." He lifts his head and hands me his pillow. "Put this over my face and then hold it there until, oh, I don't know . . . let's say I stop moving."

There are lots of areas in which I excel. As I've already mentioned, I can fold laundry with one hand. I'm also quite capable of catching the cold of just about anybody living within my zip code, I have the kind of magnetism that wordlessly beckons a guy wearing half a cantaloupe on his head to come sit next to me during long subway rides, and, though I'm hard-pressed to explain exactly how I do it, I possess an almost mystical ability to purchase appliances, furniture, and clothing approximately six minutes *before* the extremely pricey item goes on sale.

The thing I can't do is host a genuinely great party.

I attempt to invite several other friends, but one has elected to schedule elective surgery for that date (you know you're in trouble when a person would rather have her hammertoes corrected than have dinner at your place); one claims our last brunch was like "a hostage situation with lox"; one—and you know who you are—pretends to be her own housekeeper, repeating, "I sorry, no English" over and over; and two different people choose not to attend but still make me swear that I won't flambé anything again . . . like it's my fault they couldn't get their eyebrows to grow back after the cherries jubilee situation of 2005.

I crawl into bed that night a broken woman. "Why do I suck at parties?" I ask Johannes.

"Is this one of those trick questions like when you ask me if you need to lose weight and I say, 'Well, I suppose we could all stand to drop a pound or two,' and you spend the next thirty-six hours likening me to Hitler?"

I make a mental note to explore why I suck at relationships on some future night. "No," I insist, "I really want to know what I'm doing wrong. Give it to me straight, Doc, I can take it."

He smiles and puts his book aside. "That's just it; the only thing you're doing wrong is constantly striving to do everything exactly right. You want the prettiest cocktail, the freshest flowers, candles lit, music playing, dinner conversation sparkling, and you drive yourself and everybody else nuts trying to achieve it."

I would like to be the kind of person who receives this information with an open mind and a grateful heart. But my first instinct is to take my boyfriend of sixteen years up on his previous offer and smother him to death with his own orthopedically correct goose-down pillow.

The problem is, I know he's right.

I am part geisha girl, part drill sergeant, with just a soupçon of control freak thrown in for good measure. I want everyone to relax and have a wonderful time, but that has to start with me, and I'm about as cool, calm, and collected as a caged hummingbird knocking back sixty milligrams of Dexadrine while awaiting biopsy results. You can keep your meditation, your reflexology, your gin, your tonics—I'm just not the mellow type.

I approach a petite Jewish woman from the Midwest to figure out when this started. "Mom, have I always been a perfectionist?"

She attempts diplomacy. "Well, let me put it this way— you used to like to dress up in my clothes when you were maybe three or four years old."

"What does that prove? Lots of little girls play dress-up."

"True," she says, "but you tried to bulldoze Grandma into tailoring the clothes to actually fit you."

"Well, excuse me for realizing that a skirt should hit just above the knee." We are quiet for a minute. "So how do you throw a really fun party?" She reminds me that they used to hire Magical Marv for my birthdays. I remind her that Magical Marv chain-smoked and seemed to hate children.

"Yes, that's what your dad and I always enjoyed most about him," she deadpans. "Anyway, the only thing I know about giving a party is that we can never get the extra leaf into the dining table and I usually forget to serve at least one of the side dishes."

This leads me to a new theory. "Maybe bad parties are hereditary, like green eyes and diabetes," I say to Johannes.

"Okay, that's it," he announces, grabbing the phone. Before I can lunge at him, he has dialed our neighbors Paul and Cheryl and invited them to come for dinner "in about fifteen minutes."

"Are you insane?" I shriek as I stuff everything littering the floor and coffee table under the sofa. "This is grounds for divorce," I bellow, only to be reminded that we never

SOMEONE WILL BE WITH YOU SHORTLY

got married. "That's because I don't know how to throw a wedding," I hiss as I pull off my stained Sunday night yoga pants and rummage through the laundry bag for my slightly less stained Saturday afternoon yoga pants, marveling all the while at the fact that I don't do yoga.

Needless to say, Cheryl and Paul are four minutes early. "Hey, guys, can I offer you . . ." I do a quick scan of the refrigerator, "a dollop of mayonnaise?" I have hit rock bottom. Somewhere Martha Stewart hangs her head in shame. Johannes gives me a hug. There is no place to go but up. Our neighbors split a diet Snapple, we order in Thai food and proceed to talk and laugh and pass chicken satay for three straight hours.

What can I say? It is, to date, our most successful dinner party.

WHAT TO EXPECT WHEN YOU'RE NOT EXPECTING

ABOUT THREE WEEKS AFTER my daughter, Julia, was born, I was standing in line at Russ & Daughters, a lovely little shoebox of a shop that's been serving the most exquisite Jewish delicacies ever since Mr. Russ loaded up his pushcart and headed for the Lower East Side of Manhattan in 1908. I was ordering smoked butterfish and nova, sliced thinner than angel wings, as the guys behind the counter plied me with samples of apricot strudel and raspberry rugelach. It was spring, my baby was healthy, Russ & Daughters had just put out their marble nut halvah, and all was right with the world.

I was experiencing what the late, great Spalding Gray used to call "a perfect moment." Please note, Mr. Gray didn't talk about perfect days, he didn't even refer to a perfect half-hour stretch. Nope, he only suggested that there are moments when life is inexorably sweet, but those moments are few and far between—and generally over before you can capture them on the teeny camera in your ridiculously tricked-out cell phone.

The little old lady to my left decided to strike up a conversation. "So, how long have you been coming here, dear?" She smelled like Pond's cold cream and cinnamon, and I liked her immediately. "Well, ma'am, my aunt Bernice first brought me here when I was just a kid," I answered between bites. She smiled warmly and told me she grew up right around the corner, on Orchard Street, and had shopped here since the 1920s. "I raised five children on this food," she said, pointing to the baked blueberry farmer's cheese. We were soul mates in sable, partners in pickled herring; we spoke the language of lox. And that's when it happened.

My new buddy suddenly reached out her bony little liver-spotted hand, patted my baby-free middle, and asked the one question nobody should ever ask: "When are you due?"

I toyed with the possibility that she had some sort of death wish. Perhaps the question was actually a thinly veiled plea. I mean, isn't it plausible that what she was really saying was "I want to go out on a high note, so I'll just have a taste of chopped liver, and then do something so heinous that it drives this perfectly reasonable woman to club me to death with a side of salmon"?

You see, there are certain questions that must never be asked:

1. Has your surprise party happened yet?

2. How did you first learn that your husband is cheating?

And, above all:

3. When are you due?

I don't care if the woman you're asking is wearing a T-shirt with a giant rhinestone-encrusted arrow that points to her belly and reads BABY ON BOARD. I don't care if she's writhing on a gurney in the birthing room of Mount Sinai Hospital, screaming for an epidural as an obstetrician announces, "One more push and the baby will be out!" You never, let me repeat, never, ever, under any circumstances, ask a woman when she's due.

"June," I replied.

Some people collect coins, some prowl the Internet for vintage guitars; I know a woman with a closet full of antique Kewpie-doll heads. I'm not totally clear what turned her against everything from the neck down—she may have been frightened by a Barbie breast as a child. But I'm nobody to judge, because I, too, am a collector. What I collect are slights, digs, withering remarks, and the occasional mean-girl glare. I examine a good when-are-you-due story from every angle, I trade them with friends, I commit them to memory, I savor them for eternity.

Here are a few of my favorite insults:

- My old friend Alison remembers the first time she had her Hungarian husband's family over. She cooked for three straight days. The woman goulashed and paprikashed and even put her tomato sauce through a food mill, for God's sake. At the end of the meal, her new mother-in-law took Ali's hands in hers, looked her straight in the eye, and said: "I'm so glad you feel you can practice on us." Ouch.

- My former roommate Laurie came home with an A+ on her test and proudly handed the paper to her father. "Jesus," he said. "I always thought you had to be really smart to get this kind of grade." Kaboom.

- My pal Faye tells the story of spending an entire evening with a guy she met when they both reached for the same stuffed zucchini blossom at a fancy fundraiser. He suggested they get together the very next day for a picnic in Central Park, and she was delighted to take charge of the fried chicken and potato salad. The next day she waited and waited. Nearly two hours, one drumstick, half a pound of red bliss potatoes, and five weeks of dieting down the drain later, Faye picked up the phone: "What happened?" His reply: "Well, I honked . . . but you didn't come out." Yikes.

- I bring Jules to the pediatrician for her annual checkup. "Would you say she's unusually tall?" I ask, hoping that she'll someday be able to reach all the stuff her five-foot two-inch mother cannot. "No, she's average," he replies, quick and to the point. "Are you sure?" I persist. "My friends all tell me that she's really quite tall." The good doctor peers down his bifocals. "Maybe your friends don't want to tell you that she's really quite average." Touché.

Forget about kids; grown-ups say the darnedest things. Sometimes they mean well, sometimes they mean to lacerate, sometimes they're just clueless. The challenge (at least for me) is not to take any of it personally . . . even when it's meant to be taken personally. Sticks and stones may break my bones, but words will never hurt me, unless of course I decide to let them.

I've decided to stop letting them. I don't want to lock and load when a nasty comment comes my way, but I also refuse to duck and cover. Instead, I am going to answer clumsiness with equanimity, bitchiness with compassion, and verbal violence with disengagement.

I think it's a damn good plan—wise, tolerant, even kind of Zen. If I play my cards right, I could be crowned Miss Mental Health 2011. There's just one teeny, tiny problem: I honestly believe Metallica's next-door neighbor stands a better chance of getting a good night's sleep without ear plugs and an Ambien than I stand of actually getting this plan to work. But that certainly doesn't mean it's not at least worth a try.

So I will seek, to paraphrase Saint Francis of Assisi, not to be understood but to understand. I will send my collection of slights to Sotheby's and have them auction it off to the highest bidder, one dig at a time. "But Lisa," you ask, "can you really function in a kvetch-free zone?" Trust me on this: there will always be things to kvetch about.

"I love you," says the voice on the phone. We were just about to hang up. "Love you, too," I chirp back without missing a beat. Now, had this declaration come from a sweetheart, a parent, my little girl, I'd be suffused with the milk of human kindness for a couple of seconds before returning to the stack of work on my desk. But this "I love you" came from a publicist in Los Angeles who wanted me to check out her client's new sitcom.

I'd be hard-pressed to tell you the capital of North Dakota, the chief export of Ottawa, the square root of anything. I can't explain football, Congress, or the career of Bill O'Reilly. But there is one thing I know with crystal clarity: This L.A. publicist doesn't love me any more than I love her.

It's a Barnum & Bailey world, just as phony as it can be, and there was a time when I embraced every artificially sweetened, fake-fur-covered inch of it. I've engaged in that "you show me yours and I'll show you mine" exchange of faux-familiarity that passes for communication. I've played fast and loose with my inner thoughts. I've gone looking for intimacy in all the wrong places. Enough is enough.

I don't mean to suggest that we should line the borders of our personal space with barbed wire, I just want my podiatrist to quit hugging me hello. Granted, if my podiatrist were Denzel Washington, this observation would be about the importance of pedicures, but he's not and I don't think it's too much to ask that touching be confined to below the ankles. Had my boundaries been crossed by a single podiatrist, I could chalk it up to the price of fallen arches. When I finally work up the nerve to return to Russ & Daughters and a stranger waiting in line for cinnamon raisin bagels and designer cream cheese casually divulges that her husband thinks foreplay is a brand of yogurt, it's time to establish a few additional golden rules for an exceedingly tarnished age:

1. My mortgage is my business. In fact, unless you're my mother . . . no, strike that—*especially* if you're my mother, the question "What did you pay for that?" has to go.

2. I don't need regular updates on little Dakota's potty training. I wish the kid well. When he finally masters the concept, I'll send him a check for $20 and a pair of Batman underpants—but it doesn't need to be part of your outgoing message. Even toddlers are entitled to maintain a touch of mystery.

3. Let's get this kissing thing straight once and for all. The only time it's acceptable to kiss me by way of introduction is if the introduction goes as follows: "Johnny Depp, meet Lisa Kogan." Note: This rule does not apply to Daniel Craig and could potentially be waived for Thomas Jane.

4. I don't wish to mark the one-week anniversary of your labridoodle's hysterectomy. If Sparky needs her dressing changed twice a day, let that be your special secret.

5. Despite what they told us in junior high, I realize that getting pregnant isn't always easy and I sympathize more than you know. But there's an old saying: Lazy sperm does not party chatter make. Okay, it's not an old saying—but I for one still plan to needlepoint it onto a pillow. Sit down with a close friend, a box of

SOMEONE WILL BE WITH YOU SHORTLY

Kleenex, and be sad. Blurt it out to the guy serving crab puffs and you'll hate yourself in the morning.

6. And speaking of waiters—attention, restaurant personnel: Quit calling me Honey. I'm not your honey, I'm just a girl looking for a little chicken salad on whole wheat toast.

7. I'd be willing to walk through fire for the man I love, but I am not willing to share a toothbrush. There will always be an extra in my medicine chest.

8. Stay the hell out of my medicine chest.

9. You might think you know me well enough to pop by for an unannounced visit. But I need ten minutes to stuff everything I own into a closet and change from my total-slob clothes into my "Can you believe how fabulous I look when I'm just lying around?" clothes. Call first.

10. Love is a many-splendored thing—don't cheapen it. The proper response to a publicist professing love is "Excellent . . . because it looks as if I may need a kidney transplant. What say we get you tissue-typed."

☉UPPER AT SATAN'S

HAD I SIMPLY STAYED home and written last night, I might've opened this chapter with a tribute to the glorious wonders of spring. I could have said something incredibly meaningful about purpose and passion, nature and nurture. I could have worked in colorful details in which babies and balloons and Ferris wheels figured prominently. Hey, Johannes is an illustrator. I could probably talk him into some kind of Peter Max-ish doodle, drenched in wildflowers and rainbows—hell, I could be nuzzling a freaking unicorn in this very margin.

But instead of hanging at home and catching up on my work, I ventured out to a brand-new bistro where the chicken was undercooked and the wine was overpriced, the decor was too trendy and the music was too loud, the hostess was too willowy and, though I have no evidence that would hold up in a court of law, I'm pretty sure the waiter coughed on my foam-infused organic skate wing *amuse-bouche*. Dismiss me if you must, but in my heart I know that

I visited the original portal to hell last night——and I'm here to tell you that it does not take credit cards.

The truth is I don't like eating out. I don't like noise or crowds or all that arithmetic involving the tip. I don't like having to keep my daughter occupied between courses. I don't like having to navigate my diabetes without knowing precisely how much sugar and salt and fat is hiding in the food. And most of all, I don't like that NOT RESPONSIBLE FOR LOST OR STOLEN PROPERTY sign at the coat check. Mark my words, the decline of the Holy Roman Empire began with restaurants refusing to take responsibility for losing a gladiator's coat. Is it any wonder I prefer to stay home with my down-filled Eileen Fisher jacket secure in the front hall closet?

Now comes the part where I admit to my darkest secret: It isn't just trendy restaurants I like to avoid. Here I am in New York City, a town brimming with culture and possibility, a town where I can take in opera, ballet, theater at the drop of a hat, a town in which, so help me God, F. Murray Abraham stepped on my foot twice in one week. Not impressed? Okay, how about this: I actually know a guy who knows a guy who can find me authentic Ethiopian food at 4 A.M. Yep, there's no getting around it, I can ice-skate, rock climb, or take a horse-and-buggy ride on any given afternoon if I feel like it. It's just that I never feel like it.

I am part of a small, deeply mortified group of individuals who were born lacking that special spirit-of-adventure gene that makes people want to scale Everest or taste ostrich meat or walk into a Barnes & Noble without a little mascara. I still remember the day Johannes admitted that if he had the opportunity to go into outer space, free of charge, safe as can be, he'd probably just rent *Apollo 13*. I believe the exact quote was "I mean, I don't even like going upstairs."

You know how you're perfectly content with a man for long stretches and then one day he gives you his last piece of tangerine, or he spends forty minutes teaching your addled aunt Evie how to work her DVD player, or he perfects his imitation of a wombat sneezing and you just fall madly in love with him all over again? The day Johannes told me he had virtually no desire to go into outer space is the day I knew I was a goner.

There's an old Irish proverb—something about how you should work as if you don't need the money, love as if you've never been hurt, dance as if nobody's watching. I think there's much to be said for that sort of free-spirited bravado. But here's the thing: I do need the money, I have been hurt, and I won't dance—don't ask me.

For what it's worth, I know that I'm supposed to aspire to a certain degree of free-spirited bravado and that aspiring to get to T. J. Maxx before they close is perhaps not the loftiest of goals, but I'd like to make a few small points:

1. T. J. Maxx has a really good selection of underwear at a very nice discount.

2. I've decided to forgive myself for not being Amelia Earhart.

3. I like to think that if Amelia Earhart had survived,
she would have appreciated the need for quality underwear at bargain prices. At the very least, I hope she'd
have been willing to hear me out while I attempt to
make the case for not setting any world records on a
regular basis.

Dear Ms. Earhart,

*I love that you could touch the sky. I think about you
sometimes and I wonder how it is that a little girl from
Kansas learns to fly. I'm forty-nine years old and I still
can't walk in heels.*

*Tell me, Amelia, did somebody fill you with so much
confidence that you always believed you could do anything
you set your mind to? Or did somebody cut you so deep
that you always believed you had something to prove to
the universe? Were you ever tired? Were you ever lonely?
Did you get scared a lot? I like to imagine that from time
to time you were all those things, but what I find so really
remarkable is that if you ever did feel exhausted or isolated
or fragile, you never let it stop you from taking off.*

*Still, I have to ask, didn't the concept of changing into
something made of flannel, ordering in a couple of sushi
rolls, and renting a good movie ever tempt you even a
little? Because frankly, that's my idea of a perfect evening. It's not that I don't experience the odd touch of wanderlust periodically, it's just that for all my talk of missing
the swashbuckler gene, I'm currently off on an adventure
of my own.*

You see, Amelia, I'm trying to raise a six-year-old with a lovely man who lives half his life on another continent. And I'm trying to be excellent at my job. And I'm trying not to feel just awful that it's 5:51 P.M. and I'm writing a letter to a woman who vanished in 1937 when I know I should be home convincing my daughter to give eggplant Parmesan a chance before permanently relegating it to the things-we'd-rather-set-our-gums-on-fire-than-ever-taste food group.

I'm trying to understand Israel and Hamas and the auto industry and immigration reform and I'm trying to convince my insurance company to cover the blood test that it decided wasn't necessary. Let me ask you this, Amelia: Didn't you ever have to stay home and wait for somebody to come and steam-clean your rugs?

As daring goes, I realize getting a kid to eat eggplant is a far cry from being the first woman to make a nonstop solo flight across the Atlantic, but my little adventure is definitely nonstop, and Amelia, like so many of us, I'm usually flying solo.

WHAT DID DOROTHY PARKER KNOW AND WHEN DID SHE KNOW IT?

HERE'S A LITTLE FACT of life that took me by surprise: Roughly 23 million women in this country are 40 to 49 years of age and about 6,000 of us turn 50 every single day.

We are a thoroughly undefined constituency. Some of us are bachelor girls, some of us are married, and a lot of us have had trial separations that seemed to go just fine . . . at least for the husband (with the struggling rock band), who went on to become the ex-husband (with the thriving law practice). Many of us have demanding kids or aging parents or a little of each. We juggle jobs, mortgages, student loans, and medical treatments with low-fat diets, low-impact aerobics, low-grade depressions, a strong sense of irony, a dark sense of humor, and a full-bodied Cabernet.

We are tired. We are very tired—we've thought seriously about penciling in a nervous breakdown for ourselves, but we've been through everything the world has to throw at us so many times that it's damn near impossible to get nervous about much of anything.

Despite (or perhaps because of) all the coulda, woulda, shoulda moments that have come and gone, we've learned how to have a good laugh, an impromptu party, and an impure thought (or two) on a semiregular basis. We consider our options, our alternatives, our exit strategies. We take notes, we plan ahead, but we always leave room for serendipity. We are an entire generation of women who are making up our lives as we go along.

I know that it's human nature to want to glorify the past and preserve it in a delicious, if often inaccurate, cotton-candied haze. But the truth is that part of me (that would be the part of me that now needs an underwire bra and a pair of Spanx) really does miss my twenties. I still had that new car smell. I kept standing up for brides (as if they needed my assistance to stand) while waiting politely for it to be my turn. And because it never occurred to me that my turn wouldn't come, I devoted an inordinate amount of time to trying to decide whether my wedding gown should be white or ecru—by the time I hit thirty-five, I'd have been okay with paisley.

The Web had not gone mainstream when I was in my twenties, so any surfing I did (and coming from Detroit, that wasn't much) was in the ocean. I grant you, my rearview mirror might be a little bit rose-tinted, but if memory serves, those oceans were fairly clean. Come to think of it, the glaciers were glacial, the bees were alive and well, a can of tuna didn't require a warning from the surgeon general, and the climate wasn't making any sudden moves. Call me crazy, but I've always been a sucker for a nice solid layer of ozone parking itself between me and a death ray.

I'm also a great believer in time off for good behavior. I crave solitude. I like being unreachable once in a while, and in those days it was no big deal if somebody couldn't track you down for half an hour. You see, in the 1980s, we didn't know from e-mail or cell phones or Facebook or GPS, and a BlackBerry was nothing more complicated than a healthy treat that was high in antioxidants—only guess what? Nobody had ever heard of antioxidants.

I didn't need a baby aspirin every night or a Lipitor every morning. And I swear to God (that's another thing, God was still around when I was in my twenties), the closest anybody seemed to come to a genuine eating disorder was sitting on a blind date and picking at a mixed green salad until it was okay to go home and scarf down the contents of your refrigerator.

But before I start turning into my great-uncle Saul, who never fails to tell me how he could've bought the entire Upper East Side of Manhattan for $225 back in 1936 ("when an ear of corn still tasted like something"), let me say this: As much as I miss those days, I'm delighted and relieved to be done with being young.

One quick glance in the mirror is all I need to know that time is most definitely a thief. Actually, one glance and I usually think I'm holding up pretty well—it's upon closer inspection, that moment when I take a deep breath, put on my glasses, and turn up the dimmer switch, that I'm reminded gravity is not my friend. But if time has robbed me of a little elasticity and a lot of naïveté, it's left a few things in their place.

Thanks to nearly half a century at the big dance, a million

mistakes, and one extraordinary psychiatrist, I've finally achieved the occasional touch of clarity. I'm getting to be resourceful. I'm getting to be resilient, and I hope that on my better days, I'm getting to be a little more patient, a little more contemplative, a little more charitable.

Sometimes I think being middle-aged isn't about learning a lot of new lessons so much as learning the same old ones again and again. Here are a few of the lessons I keep learning:

- It is never a good thing when a shrinking portion of the population controls a growing portion of the money. It tends to make incredibly decent, hardworking, middle-class people sort of jumpy, and the next thing you know Marie Antoinette is taking a hayride to the guillotine.

- Anyone who looks okay in mustard yellow will look even better *not* in mustard yellow.

- War and famine bad, James Franco and barbecued spare ribs good.

- What doesn't kill me does not make me stronger. It makes me anxious, bitchy, and vulnerable . . . but nobody wants to see that embroidered on a pillow.

- This isn't exactly an old lesson I keep learning, but given that I've got my own book, I'd like to use it to set right an unfortunate mistake. Remember a few years ago when we all got together and decided that sleep was the new sex? I've come to believe that we were dead wrong. What do you say we make actual ouch-you're-on-my-hair, did-you-hear-the-baby, jeez-that-was-my-eye, messy, intimate, life-affirming, really, really fun sex the new sex?! Because here's the thing: Between the economy, the environment, and the powder keg that is Pakistan, nobody's getting any sleep anyway—so as long as we're all lying there wide awake. . .

• Dorothy Parker was a genius. She wrote a gem of a poem called "Indian Summer." It's very short, still, I'll just cut to the end:

> But now I know the things I know,
> And do the things I do;
> And if you do not like me so, ·
> To hell, my love, with you!

Bravo, Ms. Parker. And, finally, deep into my forties, I couldn't agree with you more.

34

*T*HAT MAN, MORRIS AARON

HERE, IN NO PARTICULAR order, is who my very feisty grandmother actually liked: my brother, myself, my friend Brenda, my other grandmother, Franklin Delano Roosevelt, Jack Benny, and just about anybody under the age of eleven. Note that my grandfather failed to make the cut. "He got jealous if I said one word to another man," she'd complain. "So why did you marry him?" I used to ask as we sat in faded flannel nightgowns doing our nails and listening to either Maria Callas or the Monkees, depending on who was closest to the record player. "I still had the Chicago World's Fair in my eyes when *that man*, Morris Aaron"—never "your Grandpa Morris," forever "*that man*, Morris Aaron"— "stepped up to the porch. I was thirty-eight and single, and my father wanted me settled," she'd say while applying a second coat of Montego Bay number 26 from Kresge's five-and-dime. For some reason the conversation usually ended with her accusing Elizabeth Taylor of being kind of slutty.

This is what I've managed to piece together about *that man*, Morris Aaron: He came from White Russia at the turn

of the century and settled in Ohio. He smoked Chester-
fields. He read the Bible. He built beautiful buildings. He
liked the lemon meringue pie from Mills Cafeteria and the
mineral baths in Mount Clemens. He'd had a wife, two
boys, and a little girl. I'm not sure what came first, but
the daughter died, the stock market crashed, the marriage
ended. He was a middle-aged carpenter by the time he
stepped up to my grandmother's front porch. They married, had my mom, and lived not all that happily ever after
till his death did them part on August 11, 1957, four years
before I was born.

I don't know what movies he saw or who got his vote.
I don't know the names of his parents or the sound of
his voice. I don't know what left him vulnerable or what
brought him solace. I don't even know why it matters
except that when you're from a small family, every death
defines every life—every link counts. My mother says he
had strong hands. She says he taught her solitaire and he told
a good story. She says he was funny, "not in the lampshade-
on-your-head way but quiet funny." In the end all I have is
one old photo onto which I project my fantasies. But there's
a second photo—an imaginary one, though no less vivid—
in which my mother and I are sitting at the counter of Mills
Cafeteria (wherever that is), on either side of my grandfather, and we're all three eating lemon meringue pie.

$\mathscr{I}$T HAD TO BE YOU

IT TOOK ME A little time, but my daughter and I have finally got our Sunday mornings down to a system. Just as
the light starts inching through our blinds and the pigeons
start making those peculiar pigeony noises and the hung-
over twenty-two-year-olds start cursing whoever invented
the Jell-O shot, Julia wakes me with words that come in a
rush from her heart: "Did you buy me anything?" And "Are
you going to buy me anything?" And my personal favorite:
"Would you like a list of things you could buy me?"

We wash our hands and preheat the oven. I get the mixing
bowl down from its shelf while she heads for the box of
Duncan Hines muffin mix in the cupboard. We hear a dull
thwumph sound from someplace beyond the dining table,
where we've set up our workstation. "What was that?" she
asks, and I tell her it was either the *New York Times* being
plopped at our doorstep or her great-grandmothers (both
accomplished bakers) turning in their graves. I snip the bag
of dry ingredients open and she pours it in the bowl. She tells
me that her pal Fiona would like to be a pastry chef when

she grows up: "She's going to make squillions and squillions of cookies and cover them in rainbow frosting." I ask Jules if she'd like to do that, but she remains committed to a career in the ballerina industry. "I wanted to be a ballerina when I was six," I say, pirouetting to the refrigerator for a couple of eggs. "So what stopped you?" Leave it to a first grader to ask the $64,000 question. There's the short answer: my distinct lack of athleticism and grace coupled with an abiding love of all things potato. And then there's the longer answer, the one about having the confidence and guts and perseverance to go after what you want. The one about the need for approval and the fear of failure and (in my case) the even greater fear of success. I measure three-quarters of a cup of whole milk and reply, "I turned seven."

I like being a writer—you get to wear a lot of black sweaters and claim to be on a ridiculous deadline when your mother calls—but I do catch myself wondering from time to time about the road not taken. Julia and I hunt for the vegetable oil and I talk to her about what might have been. "Your grandfather was a stockbroker with Merrill Lynch for thirty-seven years. He worked very, very hard cold-calling strangers and turning them into loyal clients, creating a career out of thin air and intense ambition. He never came right out and said it, but I know it would have made him really happy if he could have taught me how to be a broker. The thing is . . ." Julia's interest trails off somewhere around the Merrill Lynch reference, which I suppose is to be expected from a person in oven mitts and a tutu. Fair enough. How can I expect my daughter to make sense of this allergic reaction I have to corporate life? Do I explain that Mommy doesn't take kindly to management seminars and fluorescent lighting? Perhaps I should simply present her with my SAT scores and leave it at that. We open the can of blueberries that Mr. Hines so thoughtfully includes in every box, drain and rinse them in the sink, then begin folding the berries into the batter.

Julia positions pleated paper muffin cups in the tin. "One for Domingo, one for Jai, one for Fidel, and two for Luan," she says, rattling off the names of all the doormen on her breakfast distribution list. I ask how come Luan gets an extra and she tells me that Luan lets her try on his doorman hat. "I think he's got a big crunch on me," she confides. "How can you tell?" Julia tastes the batter, pronounces it ready, and returns to my question. "Mommy, when a boy likes you, there are signs," says my tiny dancer/relationship expert: "Like if he punches you in the arm and says he doesn't like you, that means he likes you." Now she tells me! As good advice goes, this is right up there with "Pack a sweater," and "Get plenty of roughage."

One rainy afternoon, a few weeks ago, I ran into a long-lost buddy from my days in advertising. It had been almost twenty-five years since we'd spoken. I'd gained some weight and he'd lost some hair. We ducked into a little coffee shop to dry off and catch up. He showed me a picture of his wife and kid and told me that the three of them spend summers in Paris. "We just get completely immersed in the culture." I showed him a picture of Julia and Johannes and told him that the three of us summer in my bedroom. "We just get completely immersed in the air conditioning." And then it happened: "I always had a little thing for you," he said. And people, I'm not proud of what I'm about to tell you, but here it is: I actually looked behind me to see who he was talking to. "Wait, you mean me? *Me?* The woman who helped pick out everything from long-stem tulips to La Perla lingerie for your many, many girlfriends? You had a thing for *me?*" I asked him why he neglected to speak up all those years ago. If this were a movie, here's the part where he'd reveal some incredibly dramatic secret—"The truth is, I was a spy only posing as an account executive. In my heart I knew that you were the one girl I'd be tempted to blow my cover for, and if I did that, my angel, well, we'd all be speaking Chinese right now." But this is not a movie—he thought for a minute, shrugged, and answered, "You know, I honestly can't remember."

Julia plants half-a-dozen fresh blueberries in each paper cup of batter—our secret trick to make these muffins taste like the real deal—while I wipe sticky splotches off the table and imagine what might have been. I could've spent August boating on the Seine. I could've been bullish on America. Hell, I could've danced *Swan Lake*. Anyway, that's the fantasy. The reality is I tend to get seasick; I would've pleased my father but lost my mind; and as for becoming the next Dame Margot Fonteyn, there's an excellent chance I'd have jetéed straight into the orchestra pit and crushed a cellist eleven seconds into the first act.

We put our muffins in the oven and set the timer for eighteen minutes. Julia announces that she will be using this period "to have three babies and take them swimming." I will use my eighteen minutes to shake off all dreams of a road less traveled. You make the choices you make based on what you know about yourself and what you think you know about the world. And sometimes the world will turn around and break your heart, but other times, a six-year-old will saunter in with three dolls wet from their swim lesson. The five of you will sit down to blueberry muffins, and the reality of what you wound up with will suddenly seem like the only possible choice—it just couldn't have turned out any other way.

ACKNOWLEDGMENTS

THERE ARE MANY PEOPLE to whom I am grateful, foremost among them my parents, Rosestelle and Sidney Kogan.

For their constancy, care, and level-headedness, thanks are also due to Brenda Josephs, Jan Frank, Valerie Soll, Danny Grossman, Peter Smith, Evan Handler, Francesca Gany, Amanda Lovell, Mark Kogan, Jonathan Labusch, Stephen Whitlock, Judith Stone, Lise Funderburg, Mark Schoenfeld, Scott Field, Ruth Pomerance, Susan Chumsky, Leslie Julich, Elaina Richardson, Julie Morgenstern, John Ritter, Meg Wolitzer, Ricky Schechtel, Michael Edwards, Rosalind Lichter, Robert Lupi, John Rodman, Robin Goland, Miranda Dedushi, Lidra Basha, and, of course, Johannes Labusch.

For patient shepherding of this project, I'd like to thank Robert Miller, Katie Salisbury, Mary Schuck, Kathryn Ratcliffe-Lee, and the rest of the team at HarperStudio. I'd also like to extend my sincere gratitude to Corny Koehl, Katherine Kelly, and Geneen Harston at Harpo Radio.

For endless goodness and insight, I thank the entire staff (both past and present) of *O* magazine, including Oprah

Winfrey, Gayle King, Susan Casey, Mamie Healey, Adam
Glassman, Cathleen Medwick, J. J. Miller, Farah Miller,
Jessica Winter, Polly Brewster, and Christina Weber. And
most especially Amy Gross, who first gave me the opportunity to write my own column and then gave me my incredible friend and editor, Patricia Towers, who kindly took the
time to make it shine.

Finally, I wish to acknowledge my daughter, Julia Claire.
I'm her witness; she's my mutineer.